The Book of
STORIES *from*
the LAKE

THE BYLINE OF A LIFETIME
A COLLECTION OF COLUMNS

The Book of
STORIES *from*
the LAKE

EILEEN LOVEMAN

TATE PUBLISHING & *Enterprises*

Published by Tate Publishing & Enterprises, LLC
127 E. Trade Center Terrace | Mustang, Oklahoma 73064 USA
1.888.361.9473 | www.tatepublishing.com

Tate Publishing is committed to excellence in the publishing industry. The company reflects the philosophy established by the founders, based on Psalm 68:11,
"The Lord gave the word and great was the company of those who published it."

Book design copyright © 2010 by Tate Publishing, LLC. All rights reserved.
Cover design by Kellie Southerland
Interior design by Lauran Levy

Published in the United States of America

ISBN: 978-1-61663-588-6
1. Biography & Autobiography, Personal Memoirs
2. Family & Relationships, General
10.06.24

This one is for me.

ACKNOWLEDGMENTS

On a bitterly cold evening in western New York in the month of January 2003, I sat down at my computer to check my e-mail before turning in for the night. Christmas decorations had been put away, and the snow covered the ground like a warm blanket. As the wind howled outside my bedroom window, I scanned the Internet for anything new to read. Blogging was still in its infancy, and newspapers, magazines, and tabloids had yet to find their niche with online publication. I was forty-eight years old, newly divorced, bankrupt, and didn't have a clue what I was going to do next. My children were well on their way to adulthood; my father would pass away a month later. I didn't want to dwell on where I was in life; writing became my therapy.

Bob Lonsberry, a local conservative talk show host who had also been a newspaper reporter, published a daily online column. Without fail I would check to see what he had written. Sometimes it would reflect the topics discussed on his radio show, and other times he would write about his family. Readers could converse with him by leaving a comment at the end of the article, creating a give-and-take familiarity among his readers.

On this evening, however, on the sidebar of his column was a short blurb, which read in part, "Write your own column with your own byline!" He had created a linked Web page and for a small yearly fee offered aspiring writers a chance to write whatever they wanted. The opportunity for readers (which had come to be known as "lurkers") to comment on what was just written was exciting. Their immediate feedback became a valuable tool for me as a writer. I developed a thick skin, as well as fuel for my imagination.

He called it "Writers on the Loose," and I was hooked. I wrote something *every day,* and without fail, someone would comment. Some comments were good, and others, using the gift of anonymity, bashed me all day long. Looking back, I realized it was the best thing they could have done for me, because it made me want to do better.

Writing "copy" for WOTL (as we affectionately referred to it) gave me the discipline to sit down and write something every day. Whether it was a short poem, an essay, or an open book diary, I didn't close my eyes at night until I had posted something. Little by little, I became braver and more confident in what I had written. I knew that I had touched a nerve and had moved people in ways neither they nor I had expected. My mantra became, "If I didn't make you cry, I didn't do my job."

Several years later, I approached the editor of our town newspaper, Wilma Young. She had recently become the owner, chief cook, and bottle washer of the *Williamson Sun and Record*. I had remarried and moved to a small apple farming community where everyone knew everyone else. My new husband owned a home on the lake, and we spent many nights just sitting and watching the sunsets. It became a great place to go to for inspiration and contemplation.

"Can I write something for your paper?" I asked her, thinking she would let me cover a few local stories. "I enjoy the human interest angle. Can I interview people in town?"

With that my own byline "Stories from the lake" was born.

Sometimes, I would post columns already written years before on WOTL. Other times it would be something new about whatever hit me that day, be it about family, patriotism, friends, religion, animals, or anything else that popped into my head. I wrote volumes, and people asked me if I ever considered putting the columns in book form because it was easier than keeping their refrigerator covered with torn-out columns. I had struck a nerve with both men and women, a fact that continues to surprise me to this day. In my head I pictured mothers reading my column while sitting at their kitchen table, dinner cooking on the stove. How shortsighted to not realize fathers were also raising children, as were grandparents, aunts, and uncles. I learned as I wrote and they responded, broadening my worldview while meeting head on the complexities of life. Sometimes we get the wind knocked out of us. The point is, we get back up again.

The point of all this is I would never have gotten where I am had these two people not come into my life. One never knows how dramatically one life can touch another, simply with an act of kindness. I've never met Bob Lonsberry and had no contact with him except to e-mail him to let him know I was acknowledging him in this book for the role he played. I still listen to him on the radio and smile when he regales us all with stories of his family.

If I hadn't signed on to WOTL, I would not have had the conversations with the people who wrote to me, good, bad, or indifferent. If I hadn't written for the *Sun,* I would not have gotten the exposure I received. It propelled me to write three books, with several others in production. I can't think of a better way to publicly acknowledge the appreciation and gratitude I feel for these two people.

Thank you, Bob Lonsberry, for your generous opportunity to allow me to use your space in order to "bleed all over the page." You created a forum where I wrote what I needed to stretch my brain and purge my soul. I was able get back up again none the worse for wear. I would have never taken the next step without you.

Thank you, Wilma Young, for giving me the chance to connect with my community and beyond, for having the faith in my newfound ability as a writer and encouraging me to write about the things I never realized resided inside me. They have embraced me as one of their own, and for that I will be forever grateful. The publication of my books led to book signings while traveling all over the country, lectures and speaking engagements at schools and library programs. I've even started teaching a class about memoir writing, which has become another rewarding experience. TV spots and radio interviews have prepared me for what is next. None of this would have happened had people not read your newspaper.

You have both changed my life in ways you could never have known.

Matthew 7:7–8 says, "Ask and it will be given to you; seek and you will find; knock and the door will be opened to you. For everyone who asks receives; he who seeks finds; and to him who knocks, the door will be opened."

Thank you and God bless you.

TABLE OF CONTENTS

FOREWORD

Stories from the editor:

I remember the day I first spoke with Eileen Loveman just like it was yesterday. The phone rang; it was a Thursday. *Doesn't anyone ever read my paper?* I thought. *Don't they know we're closed on Thursdays? Doesn't anyone care that I need downtime too?*

It's probably some elderly subscriber wondering where their paper was. They hadn't received it on the expected Thursday delivery day.

"Hello," I answered a little more robustly than I had intended. "Sorry, this is the *Sun & Record.* Can I help you?"

"Well, er … my name is Eileen Loveman, and I'm a writer, and I was wondering if you might consider hiring me to write for your paper?"

"What?"

"I'm a writer, I've written a sweet children's book, and I'd like to write for the local paper," the voice on the other end said.

And that's how it all started. Being a woman writer, I thought I owed her at the very least a face-to-face meeting, so Loveman and I sat down in my home office.

She brought me examples of her writing, stories about her kids when they were growing up, *George & Bob Stories: Life Lessons From Little Brothers.*

Cute, I thought, *but not the kind of writing used in a newspaper.*

She had an immediate smile on her face and a laugh that was hard to resist. She made me smile. Eileen had such a "I know I can do this and you'll like it" attitude.

It was going to be hard to turn her down.

What does she know about newspaper writing? The day-in and day-out stories, the (sometimes boring) municipal stuff, meetings and the likes, that must be covered because we are the official paper. The S&R is about school plays and sports. We recognized the little people that make a difference. We were about local tragedies and triumphs, the stuff that the big papers never cover.

I tried to explain to Eileen what the *Sun & Record* was all about, that I felt it was our duty to help connect neighbors—especially the newest ones who didn't know yet—to how wonderful a place this was to live in and raise a family. And the old timers who had subscribed for years, their stories needed to be told. They wanted to see the successes that their grandchildren were making in our pages and not just obituaries of their friends.

"Yes, that's exactly what I want to help do." She smiled back. "I've read tons of stuff by Erma Bombeck. I want to write just like her."

I was worried about my slim budget. The *Sun & Record* can only afford to print about twenty pages a week. I'd have to move the free press release stuff out to make room for a new writer. I wondered if she could bring in more readers. I had to figure this all out.

"Okay, but I can't pay you very much. The paper can't afford a lot of money," I told her.

I think she would have worked for nothing if I hadn't said anything. I couldn't do that to a fellow writer. We agreed she could work as a contract writer for a very meager fee.

And that's how this all started. Now I can't imagine a single issue without her. Eileen adds an element that isn't matched by anyone else. Read by women and men alike, Eileen Loveman is the neighbor that writes from her heart every week. As she wrote in this week's edition:

"We are all like those sleeping fruit trees ... they are a wonderful reminder of the goodness of people, the kindness and willingness of strangers to reach out to each other, to comfort and console, in what might be their own darkest hour ... if only we pay attention to how precious life is, how lucky we are to witness the blossoming fruit trees every year."

Reading that, you know what a wonderful writer Eileen is. As an editor, I am so lucky to have her talented contributions to our hometown paper and also to be able to call her my friend.

Wilma Young, Editor
Williamson Sun & Record

LIFE STORIES

LIFE IS TOO SHORT TO
PEEL A TOMATO

The question has arisen from time to time as to where I get some of my ideas for columns. I wonder sometimes myself. Sometimes they will just come from out of the blue as I sit in front of a blank screen. It's as if I'm waiting for someone to turn on my fingers so the words will flow out—an endearment my beloved uses sometimes when addressing the dogs. ("Look, boys! Momma's got words coming out of her fingers!")

When I am feeling especially inspired, the story seems to write itself. The starting point might be a title that sticks in my head or a group of words that seem to belong together. I remember reading an instruction for a recipe where it called to "peel a tomato before blanching." I thought to myself, *What? Life is too short to peel a tomato!* That has stuck in my head like a song that continues to play over and over in my mind, and now that I've used it, maybe it will finally go away. Or maybe it thinks it's better than that and should be a book title. I'll know if it shows up again tomorrow.

I have to type my words in Verdana font, changing it later to Palatino Linotype when presenting the final product to be printed for the paper. The fact that I have a column for a paper to write every week is a delight in itself. It wasn't too long ago I was not sure if it was right to call myself a bona fide writer. Enough time has passed where I can comfortably refer to myself as an author; but I realize I must always strive to do better.

Some friends and I were sitting at the local watering hole the other evening and they tossed out some "titles" they thought would be appropriate as starting points for columns. Of course I didn't write them down, and most of them I can't use since this is a family-oriented paper. But I realized among all their good intentions one fact I can't change. I need to pull the titles from my own heart, my own history, and my own fingers. Thankfully, there's plenty more where this one came from.

THE OTHERS

Years ago I wrote a column about my kitchen calendar and how it became the touchstone for my life. My children were all young when I first started jotting down dates, keeping me organized and from going crazy. Everything from doctor's appointments to major achievements (like successfully potty training them all) as well as noteworthy occasions (like the death of a much loved cat) were all scribbled across the white squares. It was a desktop calendar, like the kind you find on a banker's desk. But I kept mine plastered onto the front of the refrigerator, held in place with small magnets on the corners and one big magnet in the middle. I was able to squeeze in two months at a time. I didn't realize until the kids started getting older that very rarely were any of the appointments for me, not even the doctor visits. I was guilty of one of the easiest things a mother does—putting her needs last. While there is something to be said for making sure the family is taken care of, it is also important we make some "me time" as well. Easier said than done, I know.

I reasoned there would be time for me later, and I looked forward to the day with the anticipation of saving money in the bank. This is not to say I was a martyr in the making or a long-suffering diva. I just knew that it was not my time yet. It was still time for the "others."

Fast forward several years and the kids were in college, in the service, or on their own. I divorced their father and had a new kitchen all to myself. My calendar was bare, and I struggled to find things with which to fill in the squares. Suddenly I realized that my time had come and I wasn't ready. The "others" were gone. I was so used to putting things to the side that I hadn't prepared myself for when the moment finally arrived. Sitting in my kitchen, one different from the one they had known as kids, I realized I had absolutely nothing to do except my work. I thought to myself, *This is not all there is. What God has intended for me?* and I set about looking for what the next step should be.

It didn't take very long; with me, God is direct and intense—otherwise I don't see it. Although my life had not turned out the way I thought it would, I realized it was turning out the way it was supposed to be. The bond between my daughter and I strengthened when she survived cancer; we fought it together with the thought of giving up never entering our minds.

Taking a chance, I joined a writers group online and made some new friends. I got remarried, never expecting to fall in love again, and ultimately for the last time. I began writing for myself and published books. I moved to a new town, where I was contacted by the school district, asking if I would be interested in teaching a course about memoir writing. This led to other towns inquiring, libraries calling to carry my books, and other teaching opportunities at high schools and colleges in the area. All of this occurred while in the middle of starting a new kind of family.

The calendar is now filled with dates for book signings, speaking engagements, my beloved's comedy gigs, the veterinarian appointments, and oh yes, visits from the grandchildren. The more aware I became of the universe of opportunities, the more the world seemed to open up for me.

I understand now that it was the right thing to do to put them first, back then; it is okay now to put myself first, at last.

I look forward to what is around the corner, but I will never regret the roads I left behind.

May we always continue to keep a healthy balance between "us" and the "others," knowing that when the time is right, you will have done both.

FUNERAL BROWNIES

A respite from the gloomy, cold week of this winter was a welcome balm this past Saturday morning.

The sun was shining and the lake was still (another treat), once removed from the winds of intensity the last few evenings.

Our moods were serene as we looked out the window at the sun sparkling on the white blanket in our backyard. Everywhere we looked was white, and it was hard to tell where the floor of the horizon began and the ceiling of the sky started.

It was definitely time to play in the snow.

I wrestled with the dogs as my beloved worked on his truck, smiling every now and then when they knocked me down and I pretended to be dead.

Face down in the snow and immobile, they would stop and look at each other as if to say, *Oh no, now what do we do?*

He laughed as he read my mind and said, "They're wondering who the hell is going to feed them if you're dead."

As they came to me and nuzzled my neck as gently as a three-year-old, it reminded me of my own human children when they were three and under. Rolling around on the living room floor, they would scream "More! More!" whenever I stopped to rest. My mind's eye replayed the sweet scene over and over until I couldn't bear it any longer.

I was getting cold from lying face down in the snow, although they had no idea I was catching a quick nap. We had a date with my grown-up, once clamoring daughter, and her boyfriend, and I needed all the rest I could catch.

The sun was shining on my back and I didn't think life could get much better than this.

"You okay?" I heard from over the fence. It was my neighbor

Gary who had been watching me wrestling with the "kids" and saw me taking a longer than usual respite.

"Fine," I said, looking up now, facing him. "Just a beautiful day, isn't it?"

He nodded.

"Where've you been?" I asked him. He was retired and did a lot of volunteer work for the church. It seemed he was always available, be it for shoveling the walkway, monitoring the community clothes closet, or washing dishes after a dinner. He was their go-to guy. Years earlier, I had worked as a pastoral business manager at another church. I hoped they would not take advantage of his good nature, because people like him were hard to find.

"A funeral," he said solemnly. "They buried a parishioner today. Must have been one hundred people or more. My hands are chapped from doing dishes." And he smiled again as he held them up to show me.

"Got lots of leftover chocolate though. Want some?"

"Oh, she won't turn down chocolate cake!" the booming voice from the garage announced, and we all laughed. How very well he knew me.

"Actually," Gary continued, "they're brownies."

Funeral brownies, I thought.

It was another reminder of the blessings in my life and another chance for another wonderful day to play in the sun. Someone was buried today; their snow-playing days were over. I vowed to keep that thought in mind whenever I complained life was treating me unfairly.

"Here," he said as he handed them over the fence to me. "Enjoy."

I will.

Let us always remember to enjoy each moment we are given, for they truly are gifts. Live your life as if each bite is a treat to be savored and appreciated, because it really is.

Each and every brownie.

CEREAL SALAD

There wasn't a lot of money to spend on luxuries when I was a kid. I was the oldest of six children, and my mother managed the house pretty frugally. It was during the days of stay-at-home moms, dads who went to work early in the morning and came back home late at night.

My father commuted to the city every day, eventually working his way up the company ladder to management. It was better financially for all of us, but it lessened the need to be imaginative in ways to stretch the family dollar.

We never seemed to be without, never hungry, and we always had toys to play with.

My mother always seemed to know that we were getting bored or out of sorts, and she knew of different ways to have fun and to look at life from another angle.

One of the ways my mother used to surprise us was to serve breakfast for dinner.

It was simple enough—bacon and eggs (we never had one without the other), French toast and home fries, toast for dipping, and pancakes with lots of syrup. It was as if we had died and gone to heaven. It's amazing what simple acts will bring joy to children.

I carried that tradition to my own family, as money was tight and they were often without a two-income source. Only I went one step further.

I detested sugary cereals and drinks and would not allow them in our house when they were young. I was always concerned about their teeth. I wasn't totally draconian; I did let them eat candy. But breakfast was where I drew the line. You never saw a Cocoa Puffs, Captain Crunch, or Lucky Charms box in my kitchen. No Fruit Loops, Frosted Flakes, or Sugar Pops.

Until I realized I should take a page from my mother's book. It was time for a change.

Not only would there be the nights where we had breakfast for dinner, there was also cereal salad night.

I let them pick whatever three boxes they wanted and let them go at it. They gorged themselves on the various choices, enjoying themselves until the boxes were empty. Invariably, there were always some remnants at the bottom of the packages left, and that is what they remember most.

Cereal salad.

A childhood memory of their own making, they mixed the leftover cereal from all the boxes together and indulged in their extravagant creations.

As they became teenagers, I loosened the grips of food choices available to them. After all, one learns they have to pick their battles when dealing with people who have hormones raging through their bodies.

The funny thing was, they didn't seem to care much about it—they would rather eat the traditional breakfasts and forego the available treats.

In fact, I don't think I bought sweet cereal again until I was on my own, many, many years later. They've become a comfort food of sorts, and when I reach for them I am transported back to when my kids were little, wishing they could eat what they saw on TV instead of boring bacon and eggs, pancakes and home fries, and raisin toast for dipping.

When the wind is howling and the snow is blowing outside my window, I settle down with a bowl full of my own dirty little secret and remember a simpler time and place.

Cocoa Puffs.

YOU MAKE ME FEEL LIKE DANCING

The month of June brings graduations, weddings, and Father's Day. It is also the month of dance recitals, and for the uninitiated, it can be a time of nostalgia, family fun, and excitement.

And horror.

As I sat in the school auditorium where I had sat so many years before, I settled into my seat to watch my granddaughter, the child of my son, who also sat back into his chair. He had no idea what to expect, and I wanted to prepare him.

Then I thought about the times he and his brothers tortured me while we sat watching his sister perform. I thought I'd wait and revel in the sweet revenge I was about to experience.

It seems like only yesterday I was shepherding my youngest daughter to dance class.

From the time she could walk on her own, every Saturday morning she would bound out to the car, the sound of jiggling of tap shoes and satiny ballet slippers rustling against the dance bag slung over her shoulder. White tights or black leg warmers rolled up inside cushioned her water bottle and towels. In winter snows and spring rain, autumn hail and summer heat, we would travel the distance to learn the next step of the many routines she would learn and eventually perform at her recital.

Costumes were usually handmade in the beginning, until you progressed into the serious side of dance and performing. Then you were destined to become a bumblebee, princess (fairy or Indian, depending on the season), wood nymph, or jazz icon, and everywhere the eye could see, the prerequisite for any aspiring ballerina: sequins. These required store-bought costumes.

Chubby girls were kept in the back of the lineup: the facts of life are hard on preteen girls, and they learned quickly that to be out in front you have to be slender. In a class predominant with heavier girls, routines became top heavy with hand movements and clapping while the slender sisters were taught to gyrate and kick high with hands on hips.

Music in those days was anything from *Swan Lake, Sleeping Beauty,* and *Moonlight Sonata* to trendy BeeGees, Leo Sayer, and Air Supply. One was in quite the risqué class if they danced to Madonna.

They also got to wear "stage makeup": in reality, a slathering of red lipstick and blue eye shadow smeared over prepubescent eyelids.

It was on a hot, sunny Sunday such as this past weekend that it all came back to me. Recitals back then started at 1:00 p.m. and ended at 8:00 p.m., and all the girls were expected to remain to perform in the finale. Three uninterested brothers and a sister made for a very long day.

Thankfully, these days they were broken up, and one set of the school performed at 1:00 p.m. while the second class performed at 5:00 p.m., allowing the earlier class to go home, as each group had their own finale.

As we searched the stage for my son's daughter, the one of whom he is so proud, I smiled softly to myself with the knowledge of the onslaught of emotions he would be feeling. Groups and solos came and went, and he groaned as each child performed their spot. The stage had been filled for a total of thirty minutes, and she had not made an appearance yet.

"Do you have any aspirin?" he whispered.

"Why, do you have a headache?" I answered innocently.

"No," he said with all seriousness. "I want to overdose."

"You'll get used to it," I lied.

Maybe.

SHIRLEY'S GEMS

I didn't know her very well. In fact, we had only been in each other's company twice, and the first time was right before my wedding day. I think had I met her earlier in our lives, we would have been good friends. Shirley's heart was almost as big as she was. It was getting close enough to hear its beating that proved to be a little trickier than anticipated.

She was smaller than small, tinier than a fourteen-year-old boy. Her voice was deep and gravelly, the true sign of a smoker, and the aroma of tobacco smoke permeated everything she wore, even defying the perfectly coiffed hairdo. I had come across this personality before—it was my father all over again, a gentle soul who loved cigarettes and would not stop smoking, even though he knew the risks were great.

She was my husband's stepmother, and even though they had not spoken for a while, it was a grand homecoming when he called to tell her he was getting married "right in the middle of the pig roast …" She laughed and said she would be there, as his joy was contagious. Youth, misunderstanding, and anguish sometimes stand in the way of forming deeper relationships; this was a perfect opportunity for the both of them to connect again.

After the first wedding visit, she was coerced into coming back out "to the country" and to enjoy the summer breezes wafting off the lake. It was a pleasurable visit and a lot of memories were discussed: escapades of my husband's youth made live, all new to me and a fond reminiscence for them. The calm quietness of the day, with only the sounds of the waves breaking in the background, cemented our friendship. Our eyes locked, and the unspoken message was heard loud and clear: *We are all right, all of us. We are all right.*

Shirley loved costume jewelry and was quite an avid television and Internet shopper. She especially liked cubic zirconia, as the illusion of diamonds and gems fascinated her. I had mentioned I was still waiting for my diamond engagement ring, but technically I shouldn't expect one because my beloved has never really "asked" me to marry him. He gave me instead a three-tiered diamond necklace on our first Christmas, to mark our time together, murmuring "For yesterday, today, and tomorrow" in my ear as he fastened the clasp around my neck.

Shirley laughed and said, "Well, I don't see why not. You're pretty engaging." She guffawed loudly at her own joke, with her deep, throaty laugh, while taking another puff of her Lucky Strikes.

Lung cancer comes hard and quick, and when the diagnosis is made there isn't a lot of time to think about it. Such it was for Shirley, who chose not to share the sentence with anyone.

After being diagnosed in November, she was gone in April.

Upon distributing her belongings between her other children and my husband, we came upon her special box of jewelry. A veritable treasure chest of jewels, it contained dozens and dozens of earrings and watches, necklaces and pins, purchased and admired over the years.

Opening up the last of the boxes, I saw her trove of rings: sparkling diamonds and rubies, colorful jade and glass. To the untrained eye, they looked as real as any gems unearthed from a jeweler's case. I went through them, one by one, imaging her joy and appreciating the beauty she must have felt when trying them on. I closed the lid when I was finished, moving to other areas of the house to see what I could do to help.

Imagine my surprise when I turned to find her daughter-in-law, smiling a sad smile of acceptance and resolve, handing to me the jewelry box of gemstones.

"Take them," she said in a voice that offered no negotiation. "She would have wanted you to have them."

The weather for this week is bleak and dreary. A winter storm watch predicted in the midst of April blossoms seems abnormal and almost cruel. But while I sit at the kitchen table and organize my newfound treasures, I am oblivious to the starkness of this cold and wet Sunday afternoon.

The sparkling diamonds are a testament to the beauty of one's imagination and the healing power of acceptance. I will wear them proudly, one by one as the occasion permits.

If asked when I came into such an inheritance of cash to be able to afford such a dazzling array of gems, I will smile and raise my eyes to heaven, knowing she is watching and smiling herself.

No one need know they are not the real things. To Shirley, they were as real as any diamonds found off the coast of Africa; her spirit of the gemstones will shine on forever brightly on me.

MUD PIES ON CHINA

One of the great but simple joys we share is truly simple.

Walking.

Either alone, or with the dogs, or together, it is something done most every day, weather permitting. It's good exercise for us and very cathartic.

It's a time when we can both talk nonstop to share what's on one's own mind.

Or it can be a time of silence, where one doesn't have to worry the other is thinking, *What's wrong? She's not talking!*

More is said at those times without ever opening our mouths.

Besides the lake in front yard, there are acres and acres of open land, peppered with apple orchards. The aroma in the fall is breathtaking and pungent with the smell of ripe apples and burning wood. The summer breezes blow sweet flower fragrances through the house, and the winter winds greet us with the intensity of long held lust.

But this is spring, and spring brings its very own rewards.

Mud.

Mud is everywhere, preparing the way for green grass and tulips, softening the rough edges of the lake made raw by the ice.

Mud.

There is a pair of boots I wear only for these walks, which become more like treks, the first time we start on our journey. Special too is the jacket I don when the air is still chilled but the sun is warming as we gear up: his navy pea coat, blue with red arm stripes, fashioned especially for me. Cut and tailored, it is the coat I go walking in with him and the coat the dogs seem to think it's okay to jump up on to steal a kiss whenever they think I'm not looking.

It is. For whenever I look down and see the caked mud remnants on my coat sleeves or smack mud-encrusted boots together before I enter the house, I am reminded of another time, not so long ago.

"Here, Ma, try this," says a little voice, full of mischievous undertone.

"What is it?" I ask, playing along. It is a ritual that began when they could first put shovel to dirt in their own little backyards, so long ago.

"It's a pie!" screams the very littlest one, unable to stand the suspense, not having learned yet how to play along.

I open my mouth wide to let in the dirty spoonful of wet mud, fashioned on plates they sneaked from the kitchen. China plates that were to be used only on holidays, used now to present their greatest culinary creation, an offering of love on a chilly spring afternoon.

"No!" All laughing in unison, they save me from the concoction. "They're mud! Mud pies!" And they run off with china dishes held securely in their grasp, heading back to the mud hole beneath the giant oak tree they always played under.

Walking with my beloved, I spy the mud pushed up against a barn. I walk up and scoop up a piece, flattening it between my gloved hands.

It feels just like I remember.

"Here," I say, offering it to him. "Take a bite."

He smiles while opening his mouth wide.

Because he knows about the mud pies on china.

And I say another prayer once more, giving thanks for the blessings.

ANOTHER KIND OF JELLY

I was always one of those picky eaters when I was a kid. I marvel to this day at my mother's patience to indulge me in whatever my fussy palate would tolerate. I certainly didn't do that for my kids. In fact, there were only two choices on the table at dinnertime.

Take it or leave it.

But there was a phase where the only thing that I would eat for lunch was peanut butter and jelly, strawberry jelly to be specific.

Day after day, year after year, she would try to sneak in a tuna sandwich or maybe bologna. Sometimes I would relinquish and settle for a turkey sandwich.

But I always fell back to the old, reliable peanut butter and jelly.

Even when I started school, I asked that she pack my old standard. It was comforting to know it was there in the paper bag, along with a Twinkie and a YooHoo.

As is inevitable, as we grow older we are subjected to other ways of thinking. We are challenged to broaden our outlook on life and try new things, awaken our taste buds.

My best friend when I was younger was Jewish. We shared the same name, only her mother spelled it with the letter I instead of an E.

So it was kind of the same but different.

As was her way of going to church. She didn't. She went to Temple, and it was on Saturdays, not Sunday like *real* church.

It was kind of the same but different.

It was in the lunchroom one fall afternoon that I had my first experience in trying new things, as well as broadening my outlook, letting life come into my safe little cocoon.

We sat side by side, Eileen with an I and me, as we opened our paper bags for lunch. Her mother always packed her sandwich but threw in some matzos on the side. She always had apple juice too, where I had milk. Reaching into her sack, she pulled out her sandwich.

"What do you have?" she asked me, peering inside my bag.

"Peanut butter and jelly," I answered as I unwrapped my treasure to behold.

"So do I!" She presented hers to me. "Let's switch!"

I thought about it a moment and then thought, *What the heck.* It was, after all, peanut butter and jelly.

Taking the two pieces of bread sliced diagonally, I looked at the meal before diving right in.

As soon as I bit down to chew, I realized the texture and firmness of the bread was different. But the most surprising thing was the taste.

It was kind of the same but different.

"What kind of jelly is this?" I asked her, peanut butter sticking to the roof of my mouth.

"Grape," she said simply, enjoying her new treasure as well. "Grape jelly."

It was delicious. I didn't think I could like peanut butter and jelly any more than I did, but this was such a different taste than what I was used to. Another way of indulging in what I loved.

I thought about that jelly sandwich today at church. The church where I now worship celebrates the body and bread of Christ in a little different fashion than I am accustomed.

They use grape juice instead of wine, bread instead of wafers.

Kind of the same—but definitely different.

I know the next few years will be filled with the continuing growth and expansion of my faith.

Like strawberry versus grape, Catholic versus Jewish, and city versus rural, we're all in this together.

Don't be afraid to take a bite of life in a different way.

MOTHER NATURE'S HANDBAG

Ice chunks are floating to the surface of the lake this morning—but the sun is shining bright and hot. I imagine they will be gone by this afternoon.

For as cold as it is outside, the telltale signs of spring are everywhere. The sunrises are earlier in the morning, and it stays brighter for much later in the evening now. I like walking outside at around 6:00 p.m. amid the glimpses of light still visible, sparkles bouncing off the powdered snow that had recently fallen all around us. My wedding rose bushes that have been brought inside before final planting this spring have bloomed throughout the cold snaps and remind me of the warmth of that special day.

The dogs love this weather; besides swimming in the lake in the summertime, they love to be out in the snow. Their heavy fur coats are thick and strong, withstanding the wetness of the slush or the rain, no matter what is falling from that sky that day. It doesn't matter to them, for they just shake it off and wait patiently by the door. One by one they enter as I rub them down with a special bath towel. It's a treat they look forward to, a special massage of love and affection. They clamor among each other to see who will go first, who is the lucky one.

The ducks and the geese ride the waves that kick up with the remnants of the winter storm that passed us by, a nor'easter that dumped snow on our neighbors but seemed to pardon us this go round.

I know there's probably another storm left in old Mother Nature's handbag, but for this day I am grateful to watch the sunrise over the water. Farther off than where we can view it in the summer, I crane my neck to see it peak over the horizon, rising from the murky, chunk-filled water.

Spring is round the bend, but winter is still beautiful to me. Another piece of life for me to chew on, become part of, to fill my heart with love, joy, and gratitude.

PURPLE SUITCASE

I've been down this road before. I was a lot younger the first time I got divorced. Being only twenty-one and having a six-month-old son, I was scared pretty much all of the time but knew what I had to do. I went to JC Penney's and bought a purple suitcase to pack for my new life.

It's not that he was a bad person. He just wasn't for me.

Being divorced in the seventies was an experience in itself. Everywhere you looked there was the acceptance of doing your own thing and letting it all hang out. Some of it was a throwback to the sixties, but the environment was the same. Sex, drugs, and rock and roll. I was too much of a sheltered Catholic girl to get very adventurous.

I had a good job as a secretary and was determined to raise my son on my own. His father, afraid to be alone, quickly moved on to another. That was okay with me. No interference. That also meant no child support.

My little boy who is now a man remarked to me one day how he remembered the days before I met my second husband. It was fun, he said. *"I just remember everything as being fun."* I think he was glad he didn't have to share me with anyone. He remembers Saturday mornings and me teaching him how to do the Hustle in the kitchen, the transistor radio blaring disco music all day long. Popsicles were a treat that I gave him when I really wanted to buy myself a pound cake. His favorite lunch was tuna salad sandwiches with a little egg to stretch it. Grilled cheese sandwiches and tomato soup when he was sick.

Wow, I thought. *I guess I really did a good job of making sure he didn't see how hard it really was.* We didn't have a kitchen table for eight months. We sat on the floor in the living room of the one-bedroom apartment to eat breakfast. The linoleum in the kitchen was too cold in the winter. The purple suitcase was a table where we ate our cereal.

Fun.

He had a bed. I slept on the couch.

For two years.

I'm not complaining. It made me appreciate the value of working hard and not throwing away your money. But it wasn't as much fun as he remembered.

But the second time is different. There are no little kids to worry about. The house was sold and our belongings have been divided. I cried when I packed my purple suitcase this time because I truly was starting over again. I cried because of the life I was leaving and because I knew I was breaking his heart.

It's not that he was a bad person. He just wasn't for me.

I wonder what memories my children will keep from this marriage. Will they remember me folding the mounds of laundry I had every day and the smile on my face as I did it? Will they see me in their mind's eye as always being tired but always being there just the same? It's a whole different world out there now. There are rules and guidelines, dating services, and Internet connections. I can't relate to any of that. I wonder how they will feel seeing me with someone else, if ever.

I don't know what I'm looking for. I can't even describe it, so does it even exist? It may appear to some that I am selfish and self-centered, and this decision is only about me. It is. I've packed my purple suitcase with the hope that somewhere, someone is out there for me. I may be old when I meet him. But he's out there. And it will be the last time.

Maybe he will have survived some bumps and bruises along the way as well. I hope so. But I'll know him when I see him. He will have been searching for me, anticipating my arrival. "Welcome home," he'll say. "I've been waiting for you. Put down the purple suitcase."

He will be the one just for me.

WEEEE... I'M FREE

It's been picking at me for quite some time, the thought growing as quickly as my waistline. Dieting and exercising has become a way of life for the past five years, and as much as I hate to admit it, it's not working as well as I would like. I knew that I was going to have to throw something else into the mix, and the price of gas these days seemed to seal the deal.

I bought a bike.

Last week found us searching the aisles of Target and Walmart. I didn't want something too fancy because I'm not Lance Armstrong. But I didn't want something too simple, either, with a cute wicker basket across the handlebars. Visions of *Murder She Wrote* scenes flashed through my mind, as the writer/crime fighter Angela Lansbury pedaled through the little town where she lived, solving murders and chronicling them to show the police. I'm still a city girl at heart, and it would be just my luck to witness a crime and the criminal steal my bicycle, cute wicker basket and all.

"Are you sure you can do this?" my beloved asked me as we loaded it into the backseat of the car. We had lucked out and learned Target sold the display bikes, already assembled. It was silver and had no basket. It did have hand brakes just like Lance's, however, so I felt it was a reasonable compromise.

After giving it the once-over, he agreed it was the one for me. He was anxious for me to get started but afraid I would kill myself.

"Of course!" I answered, somewhat insulted. "What is that about learning to ride a bike? You never forget it!"

Secretly though, I wondered if I could pull it off without falling off. I named it the Silver Bullet, in honor of Stephen King, one of my favorite authors.

We went home and together we mapped out a route for me to

travel; in the event I fell into a ditch, he would know where to find me. I was to call him when I arrived at my destination, and we had calculated it would take approximately an hour.

The morning of the inaugural ride, I strapped on my helmet and slung my regular clothes snug in a knapsack behind my back. It was a perfect day to ride, the sky overcast, and the early morning sun had not yet made its appearance.

"Call me when you get there," he reminded me and snapped a picture of the liftoff.

Cycling at a normal pace, I rode with purpose and determination. The hills were hard, especially when I saw them approaching, almost mocking me in their stance. I had to get off the bike twice to walk it up, disappointed but determined.

But as in every uphill climb we encounter in this life, there is the long, delightful windy glide downhill. My mind drifted back to when I was nine years old, another time and another place, where I rode my bike unencumbered with my friends.

Traveling over hills and gullies, sometimes we rode together without saying a word, the wind blowing our hair everywhere, just enjoying the quietness and the whirl of the tires against the pavement. Now and then we would get brave and hold our hands out, three little girls abreast on the suburban tract road, holding hands and smiling. "Weeee!" we would say after a while. "I'm freee!"

A smile came to my face as I reached the final lap of my travels and whispered in my mind the same mantra. I am free, and always will be, to enjoy the experience of the uphill and the blessed gliding downhills of life. As long as I can, with the wind in my hair, I will always choose to ride.

TO STUFF OR NOT TO STUFF

I am notorious for overloading the washing machine.

It was a habit I got into from the days when I had four sets of small shirts and tiny jeans, little sweat suits and tiny sweaters. I never took into consideration that the size of the clothes my children were wearing happened to be growing at the same rate they were. The result was an inevitable rocking and rolling of an unbalanced hunk of metal walking out to my kitchen and the wailing of my kids alerting me yet again with a chaotic "Mommeee! The washer!"

Every now and then I would call Sears and ask them to send someone out to replace the agitator head, but no one was more agitated more than I was. Why couldn't someone invent a washing machine that would expand another five or six inches all around when you needed it to? Why is that socks and underwear had no problem, but sweaters always wound up wrung like a dishtowel or wrapped around a pant leg like a psychotic maypole?

As the years went by and they started to do their own laundry, I was much less inclined to overload the washer, simply because I was using it less and dry cleaning more. My clothes always seemed to fit fine, no matter how much I stuffed them in there.

So it was with a heavy heart when I heard my beloved rustling around in the laundry room the other day, sighing and humming, a sure sign he was figuring out how to ask me something without sounding accusing.

"Sweetie?" he asked as I started to think about the last thing I washed in the machine. My mind quickly went to the comforter and the dish towels and the extra pillowcases I threw in at the last minute.

"Have you been overloading the washing machine again?" And

I knew the hour of truth was upon us. "The agitator doesn't seem to be agitating …"

"Let's call Martin and see what's going on."

I later learned it was not the agitator gone bad but the fact we have a water softener installed. The salt from the system wears down the mechanisms and they simply rot away.

I had time to ponder all this as I sat in the Laundromat the other day, watching the clothes go round and round in the front loader. My new washer won't be in until Thursday.

I'm still thinking about that expandable washing machine I need to invent. Lucky for me, my dogs don't wear sweaters.

FRIENDS NEAR AND FAR,
NEW AND OLD

Whenever I am feeling sad or confused about something, I get in the car and drive. Given the price of gas these days, I do have to be mindful of a worthwhile destination.

More often than not, I sit on the back deck of our house and listen to the Great Ontario. I close my eyes and let my mind wander to wherever my subconscious will take me, the sounds of the waves in the background and the honking of the geese overhead. I often wonder if they realize the way back home or if they just get lucky.

The last six weeks I have had to say good-bye to eight people I loved, both family and friends, but mostly friends. The fact they were so young is what is most daunting; the shock of losing them without the benefit of saying good-bye is heart-wrenching for all who knew them.

I raised my family in the nineteenth ward. I made a lot of friends during those years, many who have become my mentors and touchstone, the faces I celebrate with when things are great and lament to when things are not going so well. They are who I look to when I am feeling afraid and alone or confused and need guidance or a swift kick in the pants. Our children grew up together and remain friends today, a fact of which I am quite proud and look at as a sense of accomplishment. Family is forever, whether good or bad; you need friends in this life to rely on no matter what as well. Why? Because friends remind you who you really are and they like you anyway.

Fate had it that I would journey to Pultneyville, a place as foreign to me as if moving to another country. There is such history here among the inhabitants, everyone knows everyone else, and I wondered if I would ever fit in.

Many years ago I found a sampler while flipping through the dozens of catalogues I got in the mail every month. "To Have a Friend, You Must Be a Friend," it read, and I never forgot it. I realized that having a friend does not come easily for some people, and being a friend is sometimes very hard work.

Being a friend means standing shoulder-to-shoulder with someone whose burdens have become heavy. Without saying a word you can shift some of the weight for just a little while, until they are better able to withstand the storm. Being a friend means you are willing to withstand the buffeting pellets of dissension or confusion; they do, however, sometimes feel like boulders. A friend will lift the spirits of those who need lifting without murmuring a sentence; they will know what's in your heart simply because you are there.

So although I travel back to the city from time to time to reconnect with those who have helped form me, I realize that I see the faces of new friends all around me. It is in the eyes of those with whom I pray and sing. It is in the faces of the firefighters who pass me on the road and the loved ones who stand behind them as they wait their return. It is in the smile of the one who packs my groceries and who hands me the flowers I will plant in my garden. From the shopkeeper, to the restaurateur, to the ladies who gather at house parties or backyard barbeques, I await the call to be the one who listens to them when they need it.

My heart aches for the ones I have lost and did not get to bid farewell. I know that I will see them again someday, and I try not to be too sad until that great homecoming.

Like the geese, I got lucky and realized the way home here on earth and where it is. It is here on the lake and in the city. Home is wherever my friends are.

MRS. MAGILLICUDDY IN BROOKLYN

The flight was an hour, a stress-free, smooth adventure into the surreal, and I arrived at JFK Airport in New York City with no troubles at all. Walking slowly and with measured excitement, I looked for the shuttle bus I had booked the week before that was supposed to deliver me to my hotel in Brooklyn.

After waiting thirty minutes, I called the shuttle service to figure out what was happening. Perhaps I was waiting in the wrong area, which I thought was a real possibility since the airport is one of the largest in the world. The sun was shining, the temperature a pleasant seventy-eight degrees, and I was looking forward to taking a nice cool shower in my hotel room.

"No, you're at the right place," said the woman on the other end of the line, the prerequisite Brooklyneeze accent intact.

"We just ain't going to Brooklyn today."

"Come again?" I asked. "Did you say you're not going to Brooklyn today?" My excitement quickly switched to incredulousness; after all, I had paid for a ride. What the heck was going on?

"Nah. Reverend Al Sharpton and all the demonstrators, ya know? Those guys are tying up traffic everywhere, so we figured, 'Eh? Why bother?' since we'd be losing money just sittin' on the parkway. So no—we ain't going to Brooklyn today."

The phone went dead. Welcome home, Mrs. Magillicuddy.

Mrs. Magillicuddy was what my uncle called me when I was little and living in the suburbs of Long Island. Driving to Brooklyn to visit the relatives was a weekly Sunday tradition, and I never tired of it. Viewing the emerging high-rise buildings over the horizon, I imagined one day I would work in Manhattan and maybe even live in one of them. For the meantime, I would have to be content to sit with my grandparents, my aunt and uncle, and their only daughter, my cousin.

After walking up and down the taxi lanes, I finally found a car service that was willing to go to Brooklyn that day, and my rescuer was in the form of a seventy-seven-year-old bull of a man—Rosario.

"You shoulda write abouta me. Man do I gotta story," he said in broken English. He had asked me why I was in New York City, and I told him I was a writer, attending a book signing at the Barnes and Nobles on Court Street.

"Let's a ride around for a while, 'til those people break up," he said, referring to the Al Sharpton brigade. "I no a charge you for the ride." He was right. He had a helluva story. One of these days I might even write it. But for now, I was concentrating on the stories I had written for my children, so many, many years ago.

Arriving at the Barnes and Noble later the next evening, I was pleasantly surprised to see my face and my name in big, bold letters on specially made posters and displays, which held piles of copies of my book.

"Welcome our guest author, Eileen Loveman," the manager said as I stood to speak into the microphone. I still couldn't believe I was standing in a bookstore about to read what I had written to an audience that inhabited a two-story building and would be listening to me read as they shopped or drank their coffee in the Starbucks section. I don't know how many books were sold that night or if I even sold any at all. But I was working and in Barnes and Nobles in Brooklyn. Just like I had dreamed.

Welcome home, Mrs. Magillicuddy. Indeed.

JUST THIS SIDE OF AMAZING—
WE LITTLE BALLERINAS

Exercising has never been one of my favorite things to do. In fact, I hated it up until a year ago.

No longer able to blame my extra girth on baby weight (my youngest is twenty-five years old), I realized with a heavy heart that my belly was not going to go down on its own, and the only thing following me was my rear end.

The exercise club I belonged to had everything the health-conscious woman would want. Weight machines, treadmills, rowing machines—it was a muscle addict's dream. Step and aerobic classes consisted of anything from beginner, expert, and that's okay I'll stand here in the back row.

I was able to keep up, but I wasn't happy. I couldn't wait for the class to be over and kept a constant eye on the clock. Spinning class wasn't much better. Picture rows and rows of stationary bikes filled with red-faced people going nowhere. Not my idea of a good time.

I was just about ready to give up when I spied a new class being offered. It was named PIYO, which was a combination of Pilates and yoga class.

I had no idea what this class was going to be like, but I was in for the surprise of my life.

I absolutely loved it. The instructor was classically trained in ballet and dance, a seasoned performer, a fact that was surprising given her young twenty-something age.

She was magnificent.

Starting slowly, we learned to do plies, stretches, and other ballet movements. We felt like little ballerinas. There we were, our arms above our heads, elegant rows of women who gently swept the ground with our hands, in time with the beat of a John Mayer ballad.

We watched her, all of us, as she taught us how to bend our bodies into yoga positions we had long forgotten, able to stretch farther than we ever thought possible. Our arms would glide effortlessly through the air, mimicking her.

Not content with the traditional downward-facing dog and warrior stance, we molded our bodies to move as one, and while we lay on our backs, circling our legs in the air to move into Pilates positions, we smiled in unison in anticipation of what was to come.

If it were anywhere else, it would seem comical. But we worked in tandem, loving every minute and not wanting it to end. I never looked at the clock and was disappointed when it was time to say good-bye. The bonds we had formed with each other were just this side of amazing.

Every now and then she peppered her instruction with "Suck in those bellies!" and "Don't forget to breathe!" to make sure we were paying attention.

She was as tired as we were, but we knew she loved teaching us as much as we loved learning from her. All of us drenched in sweat, not merely ladylike perspiration, we laughed as we grunted and sang with the music if we had any strength left.

The music she used was anything from modern to oldies, to 80s, to show tunes.

We never knew what she was going to do, and we loved it. We loved her.

Months went by and my body began to take the shape I had only envisioned. I was sore all over, but confident in how I looked. Joy quickly turned to disbelief when one day we learned she was no longer able to teach our class. Flabbergasted, we reached out to each other to make sure everyone had learned the devastating news. The reasons don't matter. It is what it is.

E-mails and chance meetings in hallways brought us all to the same conclusion. We were heartbroken and angry, not only that we weren't going to be seeing her, but we wouldn't see each other either, at least not in the same way we had come to know and love. What has stayed with me all this time is how very different we are, we little ballerinas, yet it affected us all in the same way.

We are at different stages in our lives, and although some have met for coffee outside the club, it was a form of friendship that stayed between the walls of the gym. Together we felt deeply the loss so great as if we had been punched in the stomach or the death of someone close to us.

The power of the friendship of women is not to be taken lightly. We know that we will all work out again together someday, and our meeting is not coincidental.

We have made connections both separately and collectively, and our feelings of affection are true and real.

I will be forever grateful to the woman who brought me back to life and to appreciate the simple acts of movement, to feel like a dancer again, and for the friendships forged out of the sweat of our ordeal.

I know this is not the end.

Just a new step toward another dance.

FLYING

I have always wanted to fly.

No, not in an airplane.

I mean fly. Literally.

Spread your arms out wide and feel your feet leave the ground. Terra firma beneath you no longer, the feeling of weightlessness and the rush of cool air through your lungs. Looking downward at the tops of houses and trees, piercing through clouds with a sense of one with God and nature.

That's what I imagine it would be like.

Never having the opportunity to pilot a single-engine craft or even jump from one, the closest I come to it is driving.

I take a lot of good-natured ribbing about my driving skills and my penchant for speeding. I love getting on the open road and just pushing the pedal down as far as it will go.

But I have found something that comes almost as close to flying.

Sitting next to him in the truck, I experience the thrill of flying without having to navigate.

Out in the apple orchards there are miles and miles of nothing but trees. Between the open road, they create their own mini highways that we can travel up and down, faster, faster, and faster still!

I close my eyes and I can feel us leave the ground. The wind whips through the open windows, blowing my hair in my eyes and taking my breath away. Every dip in the road makes us airborne for a few seconds, and we brace ourselves for the landing. The dust blows behind us as we enter each dirt road, and it is quiet except for the sound of the engine. I have realized my childhood dream of flying.

Yet another perk of living here in God's country and enjoying life with the man God intended me to be with.

A simple thrill for a simple woman; I have learned to appreciate even the smallest of gifts.

Like flying.

FIRE ON TABLE TEN

I'm a diner girl from way back.

Meatloaf and mashed potatoes, fried chicken and French fries, grilled cheese sandwiches, and even pigs in a blanket are part of my favorite meal memories. Of course, these days they are an indulgence I can only look forward to maybe every other month.

I love the lingo: "Pickup for table six" and "Adam and Eve on a raft," and even "Potatoes on fire" for that extra special zing. More often than not, I am ordering salad or a steak, filling and nutritious but not very exciting.

Girls my age have to be all about the calorie intake now. So it is with great pleasure and some giddiness that I sometimes dine at an upscale restaurant; the opportunity to "dress up" and order a glass of wine with my girlfriends is a big deal and something that I look forward to.

Ordering something out of the ordinary makes it all the more memorable. I have begun to wonder, though, why it is now exciting to go with friends as opposed to a date—and when did that begin? I can picture myself well into my nineties, donning pearls and waiting for "lady friends" to meet me at our table. Talking about our kids and husbands, maybe even the next trip we might take. When did this happen? Is it a natural progression of friendship? When we can no longer go barhopping or dancing on tables, are we reduced to mild-mannered dinners with our companions, hoping we don't fall asleep in our wine glasses or set our cloth napkins on fire by having them too close to the candles? I've begun to need my eyeglasses to read the menu. We used to joke and hold them up for the one across from us to be able to see.

Now we can't see the one across the way without our spectacles, so why bother?

The best I can hope for is that we all grow old together, needing each other to find our places at the table, no matter how long it takes.

And just for excitement, maybe setting a cloth napkin on fire. Even at a diner. "Fire on table ten." If you hear that, then you'll know it's me.

SMELLS LIKE FIFTH GRADE

I am constantly in awe of the human brain and the memories it is able to store. The minutia of thought and emotions, a mere smell or quick turn of my head can evoke the most vivid of memories or recollection of a time gone by in my short and relatively uneventful life.

Opening the door this beautiful sunny morning, I let loose the dogs for their morning ritual of running around the fenced-in yard. A giant playpen, it is where they play with each other as they chase and jump and playfully maul. Even though they are all different shapes and sizes, it is a way of expressing their love for each other. One will jump on the back of the other, trying to nip at their collars, or run around to the front, tugging on their ears. It is never done in anger, and if they could laugh, I am sure there would be large guffaws and back slapping as they race round the yard, doing lap after lap of their own Indy 500.

They learn from each other and they teach each other.

As I opened the screen door to start their morning ritual, I breathed deep the air. It was a clear, winter morning and the wind had died down. After a few days of wind and snow, the grassy area was replaced with the hard-packed white blanket on which they ran.

But it is the smell of the air this day that holds my attention and catches my breath, for it is a smell that I have breathed in once before, seemingly eons ago. It brought back a memory in an instant that brought a smile to my face and a tear to my eye.

It was a winter day in 1964, and I was in fifth grade. I was the new kid in school, yet again, for my family moved a lot. We never left New York State, but my father's job required he manage different petroleum distribution plants. The hours were long, and it seemed like he was always working, so living as close to the plant as we could was a concession my parents always made.

Although it was hard to say good-bye to friends I had made over the years, I knew that it was really a good thing for me. It taught me how to talk to anyone and how to be a good friend.

This time around, we had moved very close to the elementary school I attended. It was a move that suited me, for I loved going to school. Our house was at the top of the hill, and the school was located in the gully below. Every morning I would open the back door of the kitchen and walk down the hill to be joined by the students milling around outside. We lived so close I could hear the kids laughing and yelling, playing tag, or throwing snowballs.

Opening the door one sunny, winter morning, I caught the whiff of the cold breeze wafting up from the gully, bringing the voices of the children waiting for the door to open down below. It is the smell that has stayed with me all these years and was awakened this morning, buried deep within my psyche in safekeeping for when it was called forth once again.

They saw me and I saw them. "Hey! Eileen! Come on!" they yelled, and I smiled to myself that I was welcomed and loved once again. I think about that memory whenever I am feeling alone or friendless and am reminded that friendships are like trees, growing and changing during each season. We must tend to them daily, watering them with selfless devotion, pruning with kindness, and covering when the bitter winds of winter try to destroy them. Some friendships wither and die; others grow stronger and blossom. It is up to each gardener to till the soil of relationships to bear the rewarding fruit of friendship.

I looked toward the dogs as they circled back around to the doorway, content they had completed their laps and ready for a kiss and a cookie.

Letting them in, I lingered just a moment longer as I breathed deep the memory of being a fifth grader in the wintertime, filling my lungs and my mind once again with its sweet fragrance.

BABY AIN'T IT GRAND

When I was younger, there were three items of furniture I desperately wanted, pieces I thought would make a home complete.

First was a grand dining room set, with room to easily sit twelve. Not anything fancy or ornate, just something that matched. Captain chairs on either end, with nice linen tablecloths to go with it. But it had to be big. There were eight of us, and if we had any company, we would end up eating buffet style.

What I got instead was a nice enough smaller table, but I could never afford the matching pieces. The buffet/side cabinet was given to me, and the hutch I picked up off the side of the road for $100. So I made do. Adults in the dining room, kids in the kitchen. I served some pretty good meals in there, although one Easter there was a food fight. It was fun.

The second item I thought would make my house complete was a grandfather clock. It was large, made of cherry wood, and had a moon face on the dial. Deep, booming chimes announced the hours and half hours. I could imagine myself polishing it, setting it, and pulling the weights every daylight savings time.

What I got instead were little sweethearts I wanted to spend all my time with. I didn't have time to *tell* time, let alone *set* the time. So I made do. I taught them how to tell time by the kitchen clock.

The last and most important item I wanted was a baby grand piano.

I don't play piano very well, but I can carry a tune. I'm self-taught and play by ear. I used to cut math class in high school to go into the auditorium and practice songs I wrote, sitting on the stage in the dark. The room was always locked, but I was skinny enough to shimmy my hand through a utility door that never completely closed. I could grab the key to the stage door and lock myself in.

I'm sure the janitor heard me in there, but he never disturbed me. He must have heard the obscure melodies I put together, hearing the same exercises over and over. I wrote a lot of songs. I failed the skipped math class (at least I was consistent), but I wrote some great symphonies that only I can hear because I never shared them.

More than anything, I wanted a baby grand piano. I love live music and could have very well imagined someone sitting down and playing it during the holiday parties I used to give. I also wanted somewhere to display all my family photos, like you see in the movies.

I almost got it too. A family friend died suddenly of a stroke, and her mother knew that I loved to hear her play. She told me I could have it in memory of her daughter.

I had it about six months, and it started to cave in the dining room floor. So it had to go. So once again, I made do. I kept making do, waiting for the big payoff, when I finally got what I wanted. Doing the right things for the wrong reasons. Keeping my eye on the prize. I played the stereo all the time instead.

I've been thinking about those three things a lot these days. I realize I like them, but I don't need them. I also realized I understand now the reasons why I don't have them. It all comes down to choices. I made choices in my life that I am not sorry for. I have no regrets, no second guesses.

The three things will have a different meaning this time, if in fact I ever do get them. They represent dreams from the past, another life long gone. They will not mean my house is a complete home. It already is. The people that come to my house visit because they love me, and I love them.

Oh, I'd still like a baby grand piano, but for a different reason. Now I want to learn how to play it. I want to share my voice and my heart with the people I love. I've learned a new melody.

The three things just don't seem as important as they were before. I won the prize years ago. Take the time to learn your song, but make sure you teach it to others as well. They need to learn the tune too so they can sing it with you.

Because that's what makes a home complete.

MY OWN CAPE COD

I didn't get to go to Cape Cod this year; too much was in transition in my life.

I looked forward to going every year with my girlfriends, some who I saw on a regular basis, some who I only saw once a year on this trip.

I was anticipating the rituals we had set up for ourselves, unpacking and picking our roommates for the ten days, the morning after arrival breakfast where our hostess always left us a gift at our place setting. Sometimes it was homemade, sometimes expensive, sometimes even shipped from another country. But whatever it was, it was from her heart. In turn, we all snuck her a little gift periodically in our own way throughout the days of the visit.

Those morning-after breakfasts were almost the best part of the trip.

But not quite.

The other ritual we had was going shopping at the Christmas tree shops, all fourteen of them. Located in various towns throughout Cape Cod area, each one had the home and craft sections, holiday decoration, and food section. Each store carried the same items but always had something a little unique unto that individual store.

We'd pile in the van and then scatter once we arrived, five to seven grown women running into the store and grabbing shopping carts; we looked like children on the last day of school before summer vacation, only we were running *into* the building. Then we would come back home and compare our treasures for the day. Whoever bought the most items won the "most items bought" contest, as well as the one who "spent the least amount of money." It was great fun … and another reason I looked forward to going. It was more than fun; it was tradition.

But not quite.

There were other things we did that I looked forward to every year, such as going down to the cove near the water and picking fresh bittersweet vines to wrap them around and around into beautiful autumn wreaths to hang on our front doors. Our neighbors always knew when we had returned from our trips, for the houses were adorned with the colorful bright orange and red popped kernels of bittersweet. There was the traditional lunch of turkey sandwich on white bread with a smattering of mashed potatoes, cranberry sauce, and stuffing, all smashed together and glued to the bread with mayonnaise. Heaven indeed. Of course, being in Cape Cod, we were privy to most succulent lobster every night for dinner, something we would never miss.

And although those were great traditions and rituals we allowed ourselves as a group, we all had our own private moments alone and things that only one did to give themselves peace and serenity.

Mine was to go down to the water's edge of the Atlantic and listen to the waves. I would sit on the sand and just close my eyes, wrapped in a blanket, and let the briskness of cold autumn afternoon air wash over me. I would feel the sun on my face and sit for hours, sometimes with a six-pack of Corona beer and limes in a plastic baggie. Other times I would have a white legal pad and a pencil, just jotting down my feelings or the bare bone outline of a short story. I made some life-changing decisions while sitting on that sand.

I didn't think I would be able to do any of that this year because I wasn't able to go to Cape Cod.

But I was wrong because this year someone brought Cape Cod to me.

"*Come sit on the deck with Dad,*" Riley told me. "*Sit with him and have a beer and listen to the waves as you watch the sun go down. He likes the company.*"

I asked his dad if it would be all right, and his answer was more than what I expected. "*Come stay as long as you want,*" he said. "*Come sit on the giant rocks, clear your mind, and write your stories. I will bring you coffee in the morning and kisses in the evening. Just stay.*"

So I did.

FACING FORWARD

When is the exact moment?

The moment when a woman finally acknowledges the older face in the mirror does, in fact, belong to her? Lined lips become thinner when centering her face, the skin pulling downward from the insistence of gravity. The puffy eyes, the sagging jaw line? At what moment does she really look at herself, no longer seeing the taut skin around the eyes, the flawless pink skin of youth?

There is a short space of time for most every woman where she can look at herself and reason away some of the crow's feet and the crinkles across her brow.

"I'm just tired," she will decide, or "It's been a particularly stressful week," and she'll rationalize that if she just gets that badly needed sleep, she won't look as fatigued and will bounce right back to the face of her thirty-something years in her mind's eye.

But alas, upon awakening, there is no more hide-and-seek with the wrinkles, no ignoring the telltale signs of the beginning of jowls, the softening of the jaw or roundness of chin. No matter what her mind tells her or how she feels inside, the calendar is never wrong, and the ticking of the clock never stops.

So there she stands, face-to-face with her face, one much different than that of her memory. She can see the freckle-face tomboy that was her, with long, thick braids jutting out from either side of her head. She can see that same hair teased and curled, piled high atop her head for the prom, dressed in a gown, the first grown-up dress worn against her still rail-thin body.

She sees the short, practical haircut, a necessity now due to raising children. It is the beginning of laugh lines around her mouth and worry wrinkles around the eyes when they are older; crevices become deeper with each dare taken and every argument lost. Most days there isn't even time to look in the mirror, and the moments to scrutinize a blemish or two are fleeting.

The final realization is that time is moving quicker than she'd like. For those who have spent their life getting by on beauty alone, the moment can be particularly unsettling. She will now have to rely on substance and stance alone.

Knowing that facelifts and other remedies are only temporary and the inevitable will still make itself known, she is forced to reckon with the reality of the face smiling back at her.

And yes, it should be smiling. For although there may very well be a tinge of sadness in the knowledge she will never again look the way she used to, there are still many more roads to travel, more adventures to seek, and tasks to be accomplished. If she is lucky, she is looking at the face of her mother or one who has paved the way for her. Should she choose to walk the road less traveled, then may it be with confidence and joy to face the unknown that awaits her. With the twinkle in her eyes as the guiding light, she can forge her own path to fulfillment.

Life shows up on a woman's face. At that moment, does she realize it has and embrace it?

THE CALENDAR

I can't remember exactly when I started doing it, but it became apparent to me I needed a calendar in order to survive the schedule of working full time and going to school. My calendar is really a large desk blotter held on the side of my refrigerator with magnets in all four corners. Each page is serrated to tear off one month at a time. I keep the current month on top, with the upcoming month below it. I liked the desk-style calendar because the spaces were larger than a regular calendar, and I could write what I wanted to remember in them. I keep all my calendars, and sometimes I haul them out and wallow in nostalgia (or self-pity). It was more efficient than writing in a journal or diary. Some people keep baby books. I kept calendars.

As I got older, the calendar became my lifeline to sanity because it organized my thoughts—it helped me chart my course to get on track. The dates were circled, outlined, information written in black marker. My first college class after ten years was written in pencil. I wasn't sure if I really wanted to do it, but it was scheduled if I did. When I got a little older, I ignored my birthdays and the premature gray hair and celebrated the birthdays of siblings and friends. I eventually married, and of course, the day I married my husband was on the calendar. The day that I met his two daughters was written in, circled in pink marker. The birth of our children was on the calendar—although I had gotten anxious and written in the dates usually two weeks before anyone actually arrived.

As I got bolder, I wrote in pen! So there were many cross-outs and erasures a few years. The birth of my last child and was written in letters that were big, thick, and in black magic marker, surrounded by colored flowers and hearts, not to celebrate she was the last but to announce her arrival. I hadn't given birth to a girl of our own until then. I wasn't going to miss that one! (As if I had a choice in the matter.)

The family calendar (which it came to be known as) became the road map on the course of my family's life, and I was the driver. With six children, it kept chaos to a minimum. Scheduling doctor appointments, noting celebrations, birthdays, and tracking sick days became an exercise in diplomacy and managerial skill. You couldn't do three things on the same day. It was the record book for chicken pox, immunization shots, allergy shots (theirs, not mine), cholesterol pills, menstrual cycles, hot flashes (mine, not theirs). It held the blocked off sections for vacations and holidays. We never really had the money to travel anywhere exotic or very far, but it was noted as vacation time, so it was real. It was on the calendar. (Nope, can't do the laundry, I'm on vacation. Check the calendar.)

The calendar kept track of paydays, mortgage due dates, golf dates, and baseball games at the stadium. It also noted special days—an award, a letter to the editor printed in the paper, a song created, or dinner with my husband. The worst argument we ever had.

While time went by, the calendar was the focal point for discussions and disagreements. My children who were now teenagers but could not yet have access to the car would make sure they jotted down where they needed to be—and where they could see I needed to be since I was the one that probably had to take them there. If it wasn't on the calendar, it wasn't happening. I could tell who wrote what from the handwriting—no name was needed. It was sometimes used against me, their own mother! I had created calendar awareness. I had no defense for missing a game or a dance recital if it was on the calendar. They all knew that anything I needed to do could be rescheduled. My stuff was always in pencil, and they all knew better than to try to erase anything. But I always erased willingly because I knew one day my name would be the only one on the calendar I would have to keep track of.

As my family grew and expanded, calendar notations included grandchildren, nieces, and nephews, at the same time becoming a monitor for avoiding neglect. Since all my relatives live in different states, the calendar is used to remember birthdays other than my immediate family's. Even though I forget to send the cards, at least

I remember it's my Wisconsin sister's birthday and I should plan to call her, or better yet, e-mail her and remind my Florida sister, who's worse than me in remembering things and who will tell my California sister. Then we call my Texas brother and laugh.

As we all got older, the notations would still be written, but there didn't seem to be as many. It became a diary of events that were happening to everyone around me. Some things were important to note, but they seemed monumental only to me. It listed the proms, graduations, the Christmas gatherings, the Fourth of July parties. My son's entrance into the navy. The birth of my granddaughter. The death of my father-in-law. The day one of my children quit school. The day another got their GED. The day my best friend's child was shot. Having them all listed in the same month gives you a perspective you might not have embraced had you not seen it on the refrigerator calendar.

It's been thirty years since I started this calendar thing, and now I am about to send my daughter off on her own. She's the last, the baby of six brothers and sisters, all who have had their moments of importance before her validated on the calendar. They've all become attuned to checking the refrigerator, writing it all down on the calendar. The date is there, August 23. It's staring me in the face, but somehow I can't seem to write in the space, "Mary goes to college." Every time I try to jot this vital piece of information down, my head starts to pound, and my stomach gets fluttery. My heart aches.

Every now and then since we knew of her acceptance, I would glance at the space where I knew I had to jot down the date. August 23 had to be remembered since it was so important. But something always stopped me. It couldn't be the empty nest syndrome, none of that nonsense for me, no way! I was ecstatic, my last kid was almost outta here, and I was getting sick of this stupid calendar! I was going to be free! I started to think of how foolish I must have seemed to them all—having to write everything on the calendar for all to see. What was the big deal anyway? What would life be like without the plans for the month?

So what if I had a calendar that had nothing on it?

August 23 was coming fast, and I still hadn't written anything in. My husband, conditioned years ago to "put it on the calendar or it doesn't count," was a little confused seeing this big gaping hole in the middle of the month. August 23 was so important and yet … nothing. Every now and then he would look at me and smile knowingly, an unspoken agreement between us. We both knew she was leaving and that I couldn't write it in there, to make it real, to schedule it.

The morning of August 23 came. We had overslept! Luckily we had packed the car the night before; all we had to do was collect ourselves. As we dashed out the door, I glanced at the refrigerator to check the calendar as to what I was doing today—but I was just being foolish. Of course I knew what I was doing today.

Returning from dropping her off, I was congratulating myself for having not fallen completely apart when saying good-bye. After all, she would be back. They all came back for visits, especially at Christmas—how many days was that from now anyway?

As I went over to the refrigerator to count, the reality of the empty space hit me. Because I realized at that moment there are some things that just don't need to be written down. It doesn't have to be in black magic marker. The letters don't have to be big and loud. It's there, and you know it without having to write it on the calendar. They say home is where the heart is. I say life is where your calendar hangs. Life is on the side of my Kenmore.

I know that this was a monumental time in my life and so does my daughter. We'll both remember ten years from now that this was the weekend she went out on her own and became a person. No notation necessary. Well, maybe just in pencil.

LOON LADY OF THE LAKE

If anyone had told me that I'd spend the rest of my days living on a lake, I would have thought him or her crazy. I'm afraid of the water and can't swim. I can barely stand up to my knees in it without getting nervous. My beloved is always standing close by, humoring me and ever ready to catch me, just in case I happen to drown. I am content to sit and watch the sunsets as the light sparkles on the water and the geese head home for the evening. Seagulls and ducks wave good-bye and bid us goodnight as the moon begins to shine a path toward the cove where they will sleep for the night.

I've always loved the sounds of loons, a relative of the duck, a different fowl altogether. I would hear them every now and then on trips to the Adirondacks, and I would listen for them intently. They were a comfort and a reminder of a quieter time, when my children were young and I was a new mother.

According to Indian legends, the call of the loon meant impending death. I find that hard to believe. It is such a warm and calming sound; I doubt it could be mistaken for the sound of someone's demise.

I sit now in the dark with candles lit and his arm around my shoulder, listening for them.

I can hear them among the cacophony of the crickets, who sound like birds tweeting, the loudest bugs I've ever heard!

They call out in the darkness, as if to say, "Hello? *Whooooo, whoooo . . .*"

There's a woman here who lives on the lake and has been here for most of her life, most of her seventy-plus years. I met her one day on my daily walk with Riley, and we struck up a conversation about loons. She loves the loons as much as I do; in fact, she collects them.

But they have a special significance to her, even more so than to me.

"I like to think they are my husband calling goodnight to me," she said one early evening as she was closing up the house for the night. "He's been gone many years now, but he always kissed me goodnight. I miss that."

I blinked back my tears, for my acceptance speech to join him here in fact included those very words.

"Always kiss me goodnight."

Here's to us Loon Ladies and our never-ending quest for romance.

May we always receive our kiss goodnight.

LOVE FROM THE HAROLDS

Shortly after moving to Rochester in 1982, I met my next door neighbor, Harold. He was eighty-five years old back then, so I am sure he has long gone on to join his wife in their heavenly reward. He lived to the right of my house, with a large detached garage out back. A giant black walnut tree rested between his house and mine, and my kids would play around that tree as he watched from his back porch. He would give them a penny for every black walnut collected from the ground. You would never know we lived on a busy city street with all the harvesting going on.

Harold had an only son, also named Harold, but they called him Mike. Mike was a sign painter, and a good one at that. He would work out of the detached garage, painting and building signs. He had a distinctive style of forming the letters; you always knew which sign was Mike's when you drove down the street. It was a time where one could exist and be happy just doing what he wanted after retirement.

Mike had never married; I surmised it might have been because he had somewhat of a drinking problem. He was retired from someplace where the pension money was lucrative, and his expenses were fairly low. The money he brought in from sign painting was enough to support both his habit and put a little aside for a rainy day.

I didn't talk much to the two Harolds, since the older spent most of the time in the house during the week and the other in the detached garage. On most weekends, the older Harold would take a cab to visit his girlfriend, Mabel, who lived in the nursing home in a nearby suburb, where they allowed him to spend the night. It seems he and Mabel had been quite an item back in the day, she being the other woman and all. Harold the younger would spend his time in the garage, drinking and painting, painting and drinking.

He said his mother never knew about Mabel, but I told him I thought perhaps she did. She died one fall afternoon before I had moved there, and I only knew of her through pictures. She never smiled in any of them.

I got it into my head after a couple of months that the two Harolds might be pretty lonely, especially around holiday time. They didn't get much company, and it didn't appear young Harold was dating anyone. I started inviting them over for Thanksgiving and Christmas dinners, and it became a tradition that continued until the end.

There they would sit, the two Harolds, side by side at the dining room table, in a room already jam-packed with three high chairs and folding chairs on either side. Grandparents on both sides of my family lived too far away for regular visits, so my children enjoyed the company of the two surrogates for the short time they would stay.

One Christmas, I received a holiday greeting card from the younger Harold. On the inside of the card he had painstakingly written in his distinctive neat hand an inscription that clearly portrayed the way he felt about our friendship and the family. It was written in gold ink and signed simply, "Love from the Harolds." Touched by such thoughtfulness, I immediately framed the quote he had shared from his heart with me and kept it on the mantle or a high shelf in whatever home we lived, even after everyone had grown up and I was living alone. Anyone who read it could not recall the writer who penned it, but they agreed it was a heartfelt response to witnessing the growth of a family.

Sadly, young Harold died before the older, drinking himself into a stupor one day and never waking up. My family outgrew the little house in the city, and we moved to another house on the other side of town. The invitation for holiday dinners was still open to Harold the older, but it just wasn't the same, he said.

Sunlight and years have faded the gold ink of the inscription inside the little frame. I looked at it today and realized that I could Google the owner's name to see what else he had written. I was able to find the name and also one of the books he had written. I bought it on eBay for $2.95. It costs more to ship it than to buy it, but it is priceless to me.

Taking a Sharpie pen, I slowly outlined the fading letters in blue ink, perhaps really reading for the first time the words a tortured soul had shared with me all those years ago. Like everything else in my life, I don't see the significance of things until years later.

I returned it to its place of honor, so we can now read it and understand what he wanted to tell me. Rest in peace, my two friends, the Harolds. Thank you for a cherished gift from the heart.

> *Home Sweet Home: the home provides the vision we shall have of other races and people. It is the lens through which we get out first look at marriage and all civic duties. It is the clinic whereby we learn conversation and attitude. Impressions are created with respect to sobriety and reverence. It is the school where lessons of truth or falsehood, honesty, or deceit are learned. It is the mold which ultimately determines the structure of society.*
>
> —Perry F. Webb

CAN YOU HEAR ME NOW?

We don't usually get a lot of time to spend together because of work schedules, and this summer was no exception. A sunny day with low humidity was the signal to do something we've always wanted to try. We drove the two and a half hours to Lilydale, a spiritualist colony inhabited with mediums and those who felt they had the gift of speaking to those who have gone over to the other side. As in every profession, some were better than others. This was a totally new experience for me, and I was not sure what to expect. Would there be chanting? Smoke and mirrors? Costumes? Ending up on the doorstep of a world-renowned medium, my beloved and I took turns sitting in the waiting room.

Each of us spent thirty minutes with a slender and soft-spoken gentleman, a man reminiscent of a kindly shopkeeper in a *Harry Potter* movie, with a wise face and kind eyes. He recorded our session so that we could remember what he said to each of us, and I was thankful he did. The first person to "greet" me was Bingo Mary, my grandmother and nemesis in many of the tales about my family. Bingo Mary was the first to recognize my penchant for storytelling and bought me my first typewriter, a portable blue plastic one with white keys. I was taken aback but not surprised to learn she and my dad are still arguing in the hereafter, talking about the direction my life is about to take. I just smiled.

For as much as I complained about my grandmother when I was young, I have learned that I am just like her, much to my mother's chagrin. Between laughs and tearful moments, I was able to take away from the reading a better sense of where I came from and what I want to do. His parting words to me were uttered by Bingo Mary, a cryptic, "Remember where it all started," referring to the summer of 1964, when I sat on her patio, teaching myself to type and creating a new world where ten-year-olds didn't have to fit it with anyone. It doesn't take a visit to the hereafter to know what you want to do here on earth. But it was fun just the same.

WITNESS OF MELODIOUS MUSINGS

Where the lake meets the bay there's a small area of land and water known as the Point. Almost a small island unto itself, it is at the very end of the land mass that truly looks like a beach, complete with sand and seaweed. It has none of the familiar rocks lining the shore near our house. Most mornings you will hear the stirring of boat motors whining and engine gears grinding. It is a quiet stretch of land most of the year, almost desolate. The locals that live there full time still have to get up and go to work every day, whether it be the fruit farm down the road or taking the haul to the city.

But it is summertime now, and summer days give way to cool evening breezes off the lake, creating the perfect place to gather. Restaurants caught on early, putting tables and chairs outside. Everyone waits to sit in the sun and catch the last rays of the day before ordering dinner and a beer.

And wait for the moon to come out.

For when the moons starts to shine and illuminate the table-tops and gravel roads leading to the Point, it's a signal to all that the party has begun; its what we've been waiting for all week.

The street becomes clogged with people and cars; bikes and motorcycles block the sidewalks. It's easier to park your vehicle in a parking lot and walk the quarter mile to your destination. Midway between the marinas and summer cottages, restaurants call to you to come in off the road and have a drink and listen to some great music. An old man and his wife park their car closest to the stage and wait for the show to begin. They have packed their dinner, and the car windows are rolled down so as to not miss a thing. They sit and wait, smiling from inside their coach of comfort, protected from the sun when it is hot and humid.

We look forward to this, my beloved and I. A time where

the businessman sits next to an apple picker, the waitress rubbing elbows with the nurse. We're all here for one reason.

To have a good time.

Winters are harsh out this way, and people work hard. It's a forgone conclusion to assume they would play just as hard. There are the regulars who come every Friday for the fish fry, such as us. The old man and his wife are in the car, waiting for their fish fry to be delivered doorside. They never leave the vehicle. There are the summer rentals filled to the brim, tent dwellers and campers who want to fill their bellies before packing up their gear and moving, in the process of having their best summer ever.

It is a good summer. There are times when it has not been as hot, nights where you needed a heavy pullover to sit and listen to the band. They are the same small group of aging hippies, long hair down to the tips of their shoulder blades, faces lined and tanned from many days like this, playing for the crowd because it's fun. They have a good time, and it is obvious they, too, have been waiting for this.

Talented musicians, they offer the same shticks every weekend, for they come and stay from Friday to Sunday. "There are some songs we just won't play," the leader says from the makeshift stage. The tables we sit at are wooden, heavy, and weather beaten, splinters sticking to your palms if you don't sit quite right. These same tables have been danced upon, when the evening is really steamy and anxieties of the day of flown the coop. The umbrellas that fit through the center hole in most of them have been folded up and stacked in the corner so everyone can see the band.

"Nope, we just don't play them, because I don't like 'em!" he says, and he strums his electric guitar while the bass and backup play a few licks as well. The crowd begins to hoot and holler because they know what's coming. We can all recite the routine by heart.

"And if we don't know the song you asking for, we'll tell you we don't like 'em." The crowded tables begin to swell with humanity and sweat as they all know the punch line now, having heard it for summers past and no doubt summers to come.

"So let's just have a good time! It's summer!" And everyone raises their glass to signal the party has now begun. The old man and the woman in the car raise their glasses like everyone else, honking their horn for punctuation. The band is talented, much more deserving of bigger venues than this one. They play everything from Neil Young to Three Dog Night. When they can't remember the words to songs, they make them up.

No one seems to notice, but if they do, they don't care.

It is on evenings such as these that we look at each and smile, for even if it rains, the party will continue. The regulars know that at the first sign of raindrops, we open our umbrellas that have been stashed in pockets or purses and dance under the wet sky until the misty interlude passes. The sky is clear once again, and the stars begin to peek out from between the clouds, witnesses to melodious musings both old and new.

We glance over at the car on the sidewalk next to the stage to see the old man and his wife have fallen asleep, their mouths open and out cold. Her head rests on his shoulder, his arm around her in a protective hug. In ten minutes or so, he will wake up, put the car in gear, and turn around to go back home, until next Friday night.

They will be back, as will the rest of us.

The Roads Traveled

It's the last day of April, and I have a great May coming up.

Traveling to visit my sister in Lakeland, Florida, and a book signing at Barnes and Noble thrown in for good measure means a full week. I'm really looking forward to both.

Part of my promotion of the *George and Bob* books is this self-directed mini tour across the country. Luckily, I also get to visit with my family and friends along the way.

These jaunts across the U.S. have to coincide with my evening adult education classes I am currently teaching. Every Monday afternoon until the end of May, I sit in a classroom with some pretty remarkable women who are writing their life stories.

Talk about drama, and I mean the good kind. The youngest is seventy-nine, the oldest eighty-eight.

These women come from all walks of life, different economic and social classes. Yet they all blend in well together; they are friends. They have known each other for at least fifty years.

They are teachers, business leaders, and one is from town royalty.

What is most interesting to me is they answer the question

recently hidden in the back of my mind of late—what does it feel like to be old?

"I look in the mirror, and every morning it is a shock to see my mother standing there."

"I feel exactly like I did when I was twenty. When am I supposed to 'feel' old?"

Sure, they admit to some aches and pains, but these women are a tremendous example of what it means to take care of oneself. They continue to get their hair done at the salon, exercise, and have not smoked in eons.

One never married; only one still has her spouse by her side. They visit their siblings in Florida when the need arises, and they smile knowingly when I tell them I am visiting mine this year. Their minds are sharp and they rib each other constantly, laughing and joking about fashion trends and changes, remembering when their children were in school together, marriages, and deaths and everything in between.

Surviving the depressions, the wars, and the seventies, they are stronger now than they ever were. They are what I hope I am when I am their age.

The fact that we have been thrown together in this situation is not lost on me; I am more the student than the teacher at this class. Another gift from above; to be able to look into their eyes and have *them* tell *me* their stories.

The answer is to never allow oneself to see the end of the road. Just keep traveling it.

LIVING TIMEPIECES

I wish that I could have thought of something poignant to say, something to commemorate their graduation day. But nothing came to mind.

"That's how it is with me," I reminded them. "I'll think of something later when I sit down to write it."

It was the last Monday night we would be meeting until class began again in the fall. Would they be returning? They all said they would, unless death or family obligations prevented them. I told them to tell their friends and anyone who was interested in preserving history. I hoped with all my heart we would be continuing, for I have learned so much from them than they received in instruction from me.

They knew me from my weekly column—I knew none of them, but I was quick to learn how fascinating a group of students they were going to become.

For the past eight Mondays, we have been meeting at Williamson High School to begin a journey together. Seven in all, we meet from 4:30 p.m. to 6:30 p.m. for a "Course in Memories." It was an adult education course geared toward anyone who wanted to write about their life story, a loose-leaf binder full of thoughts and recollections to pass down to their descendants.

They wrote down their thoughts and memories after receiving their assignment every week, a bullet list of "triggers" that might jostle a memory or two. Reading it aloud the following week also brought back a cornucopia of experiences they shared without realizing it.

Writers all, they had been teachers and business leaders in the first part of their adult life. Some of them grew up in the country, here in Williamson, and never traveled far. Some of them lived in cities and others in different states. All of them were deeply affected by wars and the Great Depression, painstakingly recounting how hard it was or how scared they all were. Survival was key and not as glamorous as Hollywood would have us believe. Some have children, both natural and adopted; some did not.

What drives them all is the desire to share their experiences and knowledge with those they love. They wrote as examples of how to get through hard times, to stand tall and weather any storm that befalls them. "You come from strong, sturdy stock," they all seemed to say. "Stand up—you can do this because others before you have as well."

At times tears were shed, although it took the form of a cold or an allergy. Dark humor broke the reverie of those who for a moment traveled back to when a husband died or was taken far too soon. A comforting smile and a knowing look helped them as they helped each other, laughing and begging them to continue when one of them would stop midsentence and ask, "Is this boring you?"

"Write how you talk," I urged them. "The reader wants to recognize that it is you who is speaking to them."

One of them made paper graduation hats, black mortarboards that they put atop their heads, and posed for a picture. When I had asked earlier in the semester if I could post their picture, they said no. But that night whatever reasoning they had was put to the side when they donned the makeshift trophies. They were proud of what they had accomplished and let me snap their picture.

I urged them to continue writing over the summer because it is their story, and it isn't finished until they say it is.

I hope with all my heart they return to me again when the leaves of autumn are falling and the wheels of time are continuing to churn forward. The hours are moving steadily, and I am so blessed to be able to sit and listen to these living timepieces, to hear the jeweled *tick tock* of their lives as they relive it and tell it to us.

That's the best that I can do, for now.

MY OWN FIELD OF DREAMS

As I travel along wherever the winds of change have tossed me, the past few years have fast forwarded like flashes of lightning, illuminating certain events and situations with dreadful clarity.

My youngest son's child and my fifth grandchild will be a year old April 10. This son and his wife had a quiet marriage ceremony yesterday in a park, just the two of them and no one else but the birds, the squirrels, and a chill in the air.

I was devastated when they told me the news but held fast to the fact that it wasn't announced with anger or malice. No one was invited, not me, his father, nor her parents or any siblings. No friends except for a photographer who doubled as the witness to sign the papers with the judge. They wanted it to be just the two of them and hoped we would all understand. Eventually they would have a recommitment ceremony in the warmer weather and invite all the ones they loved. But for now, it was personal and an event they didn't want to share.

I had always known these two would marry, even when I saw them together when they were in high school. They fit well together and complemented each other's nuances. It reminded me of my first love, my high school sweetheart whom I married amid a swirl of excitement and adventure. We had eloped to Maryland and got married by a justice of the peace, and no one was there, not my parents nor his.

The irony has not been lost on me.

"You're officially now a mother-in-law," he said over the phone, a peaceful cadence to his voice I had not heard before.

"I'll be a good one," I said through tears, hoping he wouldn't hear them. "I know what *not* to do."

"We took lots of pictures, Mom," she said, taking the phone from him.

"Good." I smiled and realized I also had gained another daughter. They were going to be fine. We all were going to be fine.

Later, when my beloved called to tell me about another successful performance on the road, he stopped in mid sentence and asked how I was feeling. I replied I was a little sad that I wasn't able to be a part of it all but in doing so realized the decisions made had been a result of how they were raised.

I spent most of my adult life running from my family in some sort of semblance of independence; I wanted to do things my way and never gave a thought as to others' opinions or input. I was the firstborn of the family, the oldest cousin, and the one they all practiced on. The result of this thinking was that I raised my children to be independent as well and to challenge what they thought was not right for them, to go against the norm if they had to. I always appreciated the fact that I became the touchstone for their lives, the anchor to which they were bound. Although they still do things their own way, they check in with me to hear what they already know they are going to do.

My oldest son is engaged and wants to have a traditional wedding in the summer, with bells and whistles and then some.

"You're okay?" he asked as we said our good-byes.

"Yes," I said, knowing that I really was.

"I saw the movie," he whispered softly before we bid goodnight. "You know what you have to do."

Smiling as I put the phone into its receiver, I remembered the movie and the lines he was quoting. It was one of our favorites and summed up what we knew was meant to be.

The Field of Dreams. At the end of the movie, when the ballplayers invite James Earl Jones out into the cornfield, Kevin Costner stops him to ask, "Are you going to write about it?"

He answers softly, "I'm a writer. That's what I do."

Life goes on.

MUDDIEFIED

As I write this, I liken my life to a big bowl of mud—so much has been happening the last two months I can't see through it all, and I certainly haven't had time to write about it or hold it in my hand to look at it.

Well, that's not entirely true; I've written bits and pieces of it, not really spending too much time on descriptions. But like character development, the devil is in the details.

My oldest son got married. He waited longer than any of my other children or their friends, making sure he was only going to do it once. His beloved has a beautiful little four-year-old daughter, so I am happily a Nana once again. His father and I, high school sweethearts, silently danced together, each thanking God he didn't make the same mistakes we did. They were all there, ex-wives and ex-husbands—and although it lent itself to good-natured ribbing, we all were convinced history would not repeat itself.

The ceremony itself was short and was not held in a church. Years ago this would have bothered me greatly; however, I have learned to look at things through my children's eyes these past years, as their lives are not mine anymore.

Words of love were touchingly recited. But this ceremony was different than any other I've attended. For not only did my son pledge his love for his wife to be, he also pledged his love and a commitment to her daughter, soon to be his as well. A gold locket with a heart was placed around her neck, and as he bent down to put it on her, I now let my tears flow freely. It was one of the most touching moments I have ever witnessed, and I am so proud of the man he has become. His heart is true, and he has followed it all his life. I was not as wise at his age; I don't know if I will ever be.

Earlier in the year (March), I worked a book signing event at a Borders in Virginia, and I was surprised to find myself located in the children's area. Usually you can find me either in the front or the back of the store while this was way off to the side, next to dragons and SpongeBob, and part of a school book fair. The book did just as well, though, and I was not surprised to hear the elementary school kids ask, "Read one more," when I had finished each chapter. Memories of my own babies (whom the stories are based upon) rose to the top of my consciousness, and I had to watch the catch in my voice when I read the story of Jacob. It seemed like yesterday that it was them who were sitting cross-legged on the floor before they had babies of their own. Since I was in Colorado to attend the wedding, I asked my publisher to schedule a book signing at the local Barnes and Noble Booksellers, to promote the book that got me on the literary radar. It was the third event in a yearlong mini tour we've developed, promoting *George and Bob Stories* before my next book is released.

This event was a little different (in fact, no two are the same) where the store manager had me up front as customers walked into the store. There was no reading and I sat there, smiling, as they walked in. They had no choice but to stop at my table, and I think that was a great selling point.

The highlight for me was taking pictures of families who had purchased my books, and strangers at that. I laughed to myself as they snapped the shot, remembering when it was only friends and relatives that bought the things.

I've begun teaching a class on writing memoirs entitled tongue-in-cheek "A Course in Memories." From 4:30 to 6:30 p.m. on a Monday night, I sit and listen to my seven students read their writings on specific "memory triggers" I have assigned them. The response has been overwhelming and quite awe-inspiring for me. To hear some of the things these women have been through is truly miraculous. The "baby" of the group is seventy-seven years old, and I believe the oldest is ninety-two. This is only the third class, and already I am entranced. They are excited to be sharing their stories with those who have undoubtedly been their neighbors for sixty-plus years. I can't wait for them to return the next weeks. I also can't wait to take a picture of the first "graduating class."

This past week has also found me interviewing two women

from very different situations but whose connection is a dog. One is a young woman of sixteen who trains Seeing-Eye Guide Dogs and has won the Youth of the Year award from our town chamber of commerce. Home schooled, she spends all day with Beau, her yellow Lab, and together they learn what is needed to become someone else's eyes. The commitment and the sacrifice of this teen is truly inspiring. She can only do what Beau can do, so if Beau is afraid of stairs (which he is), she has to find a way to get upstairs without them. Either that or go home. "How do you not get attached, being with him twenty-four-seven?" I asked her.

"I remind myself that I am doing this for someone else, that I am helping someone in need. It's not about me or what I want."

Another one with such wisdom. Anyone who doubts the compassion of this generation should walk a day in my shoes.

The other woman touched by a canine is a mother of three children, two of which are autistic. The dog, a golden Labrador, uses the strength of its body to calm its master, an eight-year-old who has run off more times than anyone can count. She lays on him when he is stressed and licks his face when he is frightened. It is the ultimate in companionship, for this may be the only friend a child like this can have. Taught also to seek and rescue, the animal can locate his scent in a moment's notice, perhaps saving his life or returning him to safety should he run off. I sit and listen to his mother explain how they learned two of their children are autistic, and all I can think is God bless you; I don't know how you survive that …

All in all, it's been quite a mixture of awe and heartfelt love these few weeks. Via weddings, book signings, and wonder doggies. I feel honored and oh so blessed to be here for it all.

And it's only April.

THE LAKE NEVER FAILS

Another snowy day in western New York, and I am so glad that I work from home.

Grateful also to the man who provides the security to enable me this luxury, I always remember to thank him because he is the reason I am here. Turning to face the big window that faces the water, I listen to the pounding of the waves and the wind during this winter storm. A big pot of soup sits on the stove, simmering and filling our little house with delicious smells emanating from the frozen hambone I saved from Christmas dinner. Like the memories in the back of my mind, it defrosts and the goodness seeps out, filling our hearts and minds with peaceful contentment

It never ceases to amaze me how much material I can garner from simply listening to the lake. Dressed in sweats and wooly slippers, washing machine whirring in the background, I am ready to begin my day's work at noon. Such is the ambiguity of a writer— our days can start anywhere from 3:00 a.m. or noon, depending when the muse decides to wake us and compel production. It seems easier to turn it off than on, but the pull to create should never be ignored.

The ballerinas and I are back in full force, the group of women who exercise together and with whom an unbreakable bond has been formed.

Originating from an exercise club, we quickly realized we enjoyed the dance aspect of the workout rather than the monotony of pushups and jumping jacks. Infused with Pilates and yoga, we were quickly transformed into plies enthusiasts, first and second position fanatics ("Are my legs facing the right way?"), and lovers of deep stretches. I was surprised to learn the variations there are of manipulating your body aside a ballet bar. I never knew I could raise my leg above my head and not pass out. Nor did I realize the giddy freedom in having all the blood rush to my head while my rear end was facing heaven.

With muscles screaming and abdomen burning, an idea popped into my head for a column. My muse has the absolute worst timing, and I was unable to neither extricate myself from the bar nor untie my legs on the mat later when she tried to poke me again. My only hope was that I would remember the thoughts and feelings surrounding it when I sat to look at the lake.

It never fails me.

SAYING GOOD-BYE

The first funeral I ever attended was in 1984; I was thirty years old. It was the father of one of my neighbors, a woman whose oldest son went to school with my youngest son. My grandparents had passed on early, one set in Ireland, the other in New York City. I was in my twenties, pregnant, and unable to travel to anywhere, but even if I wasn't, I would not have made the trip. I loved them, but I said good-bye in my own way.

Tradition says we honor our dead by paying tribute to them. Attending wakes and viewings and memorials, we sit and cry among the others who loved them as well, and perhaps visit with family members we haven't seen in a while.

I couldn't do it.

I was deathly afraid of death.

Uncomfortable does not even begin to describe the feelings that would well up inside me when the mention of a funeral arose in conversation. I don't know where it came from; I was never forced to attend any.

Thoughts of kneeling in front of the casket brought about terror and fear, not wanting to touch or even look at the decedent. I felt awful for those who mourned, not wanting to be around those who cried or even allow myself to shed a tear, for fear I would sob uncontrollably and embarrass those who were already suffering.

I certainly didn't want those who needed to be comforted consoling me.

Until I was forty-four years old, I had only attended two funerals.

As is with everything thing else in life, the time when I would have to face such issues inevitably arrived. It was not for a family or even a friend. A complete stranger brought me full circle, the passing of a little old lady who had raised a family, loved her church community, and everything about life itself—the good, the bad, and especially the ugly.

I had been hired six months previously as a pastoral business manager for several Catholic churches in the city; it was there that I learned the art of mourning and bereavement. Working with a priest whose calling was truly the funeral Mass, I learned about the process of grief and mourning and saying good-bye. It was as if God himself had tapped me on the shoulder and admonished, waving a finger and saying, "Come now, get over this. It's not about you."

As a pastoral presence, I walked with them as they looked at a Scripture reading and picked hymns and where to socialize afterward. I held my breath as I held the hand of those who were weeping, hugged those who shoulders were weary from the burdens of illness they had witnessed for so long. I learned that it is all right to cry, to laugh, and even alternate between the two emotions in an instant.

I learned the one who left us is not gone forever, just out of sight.

I learned how to truly minister to those who are grieving but allow them to minister to me.

I learned to let them see me grieve as well. To celebrate and honor the life of someone who had touched us is the greatest gift we can offer, the ultimate in tribute, no matter how confusing, tragic, or sad.

There is nothing to fear about death. I've gone to countless funerals since then, kissing the cheeks of friends who have left me and the faces of those who loved them too.

Needless to say, they are becoming more frequent as time moves forward.

In fact, I read the obituaries every morning to see if I recognize the deceased, to be certain I am able to attend to say good-bye, to wish them farewell. To acknowledge that they were here and that I loved them, they affected me; they had become a part of my life. I hope when my time comes there are those who will want to say good-bye to me, unafraid and unencumbered by the trivialities of life.

No longer afraid of death and dying, I will embrace those who have embraced me.

For although we mourn loved ones who have left us, there are those who are joyous at their arrival.

THE BEND IN THE ROAD

When I was growing up on Long Island, most everybody's father had a two-hour, one-way drive to work. A lot of my friend's dads worked either right downtown or the surrounding areas, like Brooklyn, Queens, Flatbush, or Jamaica. My father talked about traffic on the LIE (Long Island Expressway) and the fact that sometimes he had to stop at the local tavern so that he could wait out the bottlenecks. My mother used to smile whenever she heard that one, for the "bottlenecks" weren't just on the road.

As I got older and entered the workplace myself, it was expected that I wouldn't have to travel so far to earn a living. Farmland was disappearing, and housing developments or tract homes took their place. Shopping centers (the term *mall* hadn't been invented yet) and surrounding complexes were the first bane of the mom and pop stores that were slowing fading from the landscape. Doctors' offices and lawyers' co-ops were taking shape, as were clinics and super-duper supermarkets.

When I finally did get a grown-up, full-time job with health benefits and pension rights, I didn't have to travel very far, perhaps ten minutes away. It was a trend that was soon to follow me wherever I went.

Housing in the most convenient areas determined where I would work rather than where I would live. Up until a few weeks ago, my residence was within five minutes' walking distance to one of the churches. The other two churches were also walk able, but only if I was ambitious. But if I lost my car, I wouldn't lose my job.

So it was with a wry smile that I responded to that wonderful question with, "You want me to move where and drive for how long?"

A dilemma at best, for I loved the man, and I loved the job.

On its face, it looked like I was sacrificing a lot to live the life I wanted to embrace. It meant getting up two hours earlier than I usually did and driving for an hour if I obeyed the speed limit.

But the reward was to watch the sun come up over the lake, the Great Ontario. As we sat on the porch, hot coffee in our gloved hands, it was a marvel to behold. Even in the dead of winter I wouldn't trade that view for anything.

Returning home in the evening was still another exercise in timing. Although traffic paled in comparison to the days of my dad on the LIE, a bottleneck now and then would make me smile as I heard him in my head. I wish there was a place I could pull over and wait it out.

But the reward for the drive home is one of the reasons why I am here.

There are two ways to travel from the city to the country and then back again. One way is to take a straight run from the bridge, a stretch of highway that goes for 101 miles. It runs parallel with the lake, but you can't *see* the lake; it's way too far in and blocked by the trees, invisible during spring and summer. Standard highway speed limits run from fifty-five to sixty-five miles per hour, and you can get here to there in the blink of an eye, without smelling the air or hearing the waves.

The other way is to turn left as soon as you cross over the bridge from the mainland, to run right *along* the lake.

That is only the first part of the reward, however.

It took a while for me to do the latter, for I was fearful of getting lost. Directionally challenged, I knew I would do better just taking the straight south to north stretch and turning left at the last moment closest to the entrance to the lake where "our" house is.

Through whiteouts and snowdrifts, snowstorms and ice melts, I braved the miles and drove, slowly when I had to, stopping when I needed, and arriving when I was supposed to.

I thought of my father often during these winter treks and wondered how he did it all those years, close to thirty. It wasn't until the snow started to melt that I began to understand why.

For when the air started to turn warmer and the buds began to pop on the trees, I turned left.

I had entered another world, another realm of existence. This world had apple trees and cherry blossoms, green grass and corn stalks. Up and down hills and valleys, twists and turns, the speed limits would vary between thirty miles per hour and fifty-five. Ducks and geese would cross the road, and every now and then a deer would poke its face out of the bushes.

For a city girl, this was fairy land.

The lake is my constant companion as I travel the extra miles it takes me to get there, home to him and my place beside him.

But the *very* best part and the reason why we are both here is the view that greets me every time I come or I go from where I started.

There's a bend in the road, a crook in the landscape that is breathtaking. When the wind is moving, the waves crash up against the rocks; it is the first thing I see when I straighten back out again. Coming over the hill and down into the valley, it is a magnificent view that hits you instantly and takes you somewhere else. We might as well be living in Maine or Cape Cod, for the air is heavy with moisture, and the smells are laden with flowers and salty freshness. The sun glistens on the water, sparkling diamonds as far as the eye can see.

It is the announcement to me that I am close to home and a poignant reminder as to why I am here.

Views like this are gifts from God. I met the one he gave it to, and he shared it with me.

So I will drive and drive, for as long as I can, as long as I have the strength and the will, and my eyes will behold the beauty that awaits me every morning as I leave and every evening as I return.

As I turn left I make a small salute to my dad as he travels the route with me.

The bend in the road to home. To him and to the lake.

THE WINTER OF MY DISCONTENT

Winter has finally arrived in Rochester.

Like one of my favorite stories by John Steinbeck, I am feeling a lot like Ethan lately.

He has a good life, a beautiful family, and the respect of his community. But there is something missing, and we journey with him as he weaves through years of ambiguity to find the meaning of what is real and what is merely a dream. The magnitude of true love and all the trauma that can attach itself to it.

The snow is piled high outside our window here at the lake, a beautiful sight to behold. Even before the sun rises, the brightness of the flakes reflects off the water, giving the morning a surreal glow all around us. It is both calming and invigorating at the same time.

I sit and watch the ducks as they dive with the sunrise, looking for breakfast, exercising their freedom.

I wonder if they realize how lucky they are.

Winter has been long in coming this year, the ground refusing to harden to accept the snow as it melts into the earth, providing drinks for the roots of the mighty weeping willow outside my window. At times steam arises from the water as it hits the air, warmer than usual with foggy mists hovering over the waves.

I sit with my husband as we sip our coffee in silence, enjoying the quiet and the presence of each other. We have only been together for a short time, but it is as if we have known each other for years on end. Perhaps in another life we were lovers, or maybe even companions to others. Whatever the origin, we are soul mates.

Having reached the time in my life where I no longer produce children, I am content to raise animals as the next best thing. They are like the babies I once had, and they watch out for me as dearly as I do them. They sit silently at our feet, also enjoying the luxury of time and quiet this blissful morning produces.

My real babies are gone, off on lives of their own with adventures and missteps along the way. It is a joy and a heartbreak to watch them as they walk in one direction, only to realize they have to double back and try again.

So the winter of my discontent this year is not really that of disharmony or anxiousness, of longing or vanishing what ifs like the vapors of the fog on the water.

It is realizing that I have so much yet to do in this life, and I only have so much time left. I will not miss another minute of it.

I hope you realize how wonderful life is and the opportunities awaiting you, only a breath away. Don't waste a moment of it.

Like the leaves of the weeping willow outside my window, I will not let them die on the vine.

THERE'S A REASON

There's a reason February is the shortest month of the year.

Although the northeast has been blessed with phenomenally warm temperatures this year, it is typically the darkest time of the winter season.

The skies are usually gray; the sun only peeks its head out once every six or seven days. Bleak is not nearly enough a description, but it's the only one we have.

Snow is a welcome respite at times from these days, for at least it brightens the landscape and gives one a reason to venture outdoors. I love to sled, as I've never had the luxury of learning to ski or snowboard. I know it's not that difficult; it was just a time consideration. I would have much rather sat on the round plastic snow disc with my kids than travel to nearby man-made snow trails.

I think God created February as a way to recharge our batteries from the hustle and bustle of the holiday seasons. Gone are the decorations and trappings of the Christmas and Hanukkah; the shock of credit card bills received in January has subsided, and we are ready to hunker down for the last blasts of old man winter.

As the dusky afternoon begins to wind down to dampened quiet evening shadows, it becomes a time of reflection for me. Church meetings and gatherings with friends continue throughout the month. Lovers who celebrate Valentine's Day are reminded to acknowledge this love, rekindle an old one, or throw a fire on the log of a newly sparked flame.

Super Bowl parties and family birthday celebrations come round like clockwork. I'll be walking in a fund-raiser, the Gilda's Walk for Wellness, a "Noogiewalk" for children and families living with cancer.

Of course it has hit home, as my daughter and many friends

have either survived this demon interloper or are fighting with it at this moment. Some have been called home, and it is a way to affirm their memory, a way to dedicate my love to them. It is a brief and vivid moment where I can help in the miniscule way I can.

February is packed full with to-do lists and fills up pretty quickly, for it is the shortest day of the month. I believe there is a reason for that.

Let us always possess the awareness of a positive outlook for the times to come, a hopeful reminder that spring is not far behind.

WINTER

Living in western New York, I am around the snow and cold of winter longer than I would like. However, I have learned to accept and even befriend winter because it is stronger, hardier, and more insistent than I am.

Winter's beauty sneaks up on you. One of my favorite things to do is watch the snow cascade outside my living room picture window during an evening storm. Winter is definitely the winner in this war between the elements. Before the storm has really picked up speed, the flakes slowly pile up on my driveway one by one. The outdoor spotlights, intended to illuminate intruders on my property, make the flakes shimmer in the moonlight as they fall. They don't seem as ominous when they pile up neatly on the tips of pine trees and bushes.

When the velocity of the wind increases and the storm gains more power, I am reminded how fortunate I am to be behind the glass and merely a spectator, not an involved party. The wind blows in the background like a carnival pipe organ, pausing on one note for just a moment before it resumes its ancient aria, blowing in and out between the tree branches. An owl or two will hoot along, as if they know they are part of a grand orchestra and must play their part in the piece. Twigs slap against window glass, adding a constant rhythm to the already chaotic symphony, trying to keep time with the ever-constant wind. I go to sleep listening to these beautiful instruments of the backyard, knowing that I am warm and safe inside in my bed.

In the early morning I can picture in my mind's eye the snow glistening in the sunrise, washed in the glow of the sunshine and flickers as the light hits it intermittently. Before the velvety blanket is rumpled with the imprint of footsteps, the crystals glitter like a mini firecracker exploding silently. It is quiet and the earth is not awake yet. A squirrel or two may quickly hop across a mound, as if the ground were too hot to linger on for more than a second.

The sky is clear and bright blue, so bright one can't look directly into it. The wind is barely moving now, yet when a stray flake blows up again my window glass, I raise my hand as if to stop it from coming any closer.

But alas, I have been fooled again! Now that I am up and out of bed, I look out the window and view what destruction has been wrought by this sneaky and sinister centurion of the night. Beguiling and seductive in the evening, he shows his true colors this morning in the damage he has left behind.

Snow is piled high on picnic tables and cars. Ice blown from the wind has formed on window ledges, and on electric wires, and phone lines. Sidewalks are buried beneath mountains of snow, leaving me stranded and afraid. There is no heat in the house now as I make my way barefoot to view the thermostat that reads forty degrees. I will have to be content to stack my fireplace with logs from the basement and stay indoors for the rest of the morning, catnapping as I cannot find anything good to read.

When I awake, it is twilight, almost night again. The need to sleep must have overpowered my bad mood. The fire has long gone out, as evidenced by the ashes in the fireplace, but it is warm. The heat must have kicked on sometime during the afternoon. My stomach growls, reminding me that I haven't eaten all day.

Stumbling to the kitchen, I am greeted by a new view, a different view than the living room picture window offers. I arrive just to glimpse the tail of a black dog running by, leaving only the steam from his nostrils as his hot breaths puff behind him like a locomotive steam engine. The dog is chasing a squirrel who now has no trouble at all jumping from mound to mound and up the bark of a tree. My eyes are drawn upward to the magnificent overcoat of snow hanging from the branches of the beautiful oak, bending it but not overpowering it. I am reminded once again that winter is the boss, and I am but an obedient servant awaiting my next instruction, my next lesson in appreciating the power of winter.

FORGIVING

An old friend was over for dinner last night, someone with whom I had a falling out several years ago.

We both said some pretty harsh things to each other, words that can never be taken back, statements played over in over in our minds that bring both guilt and sadness.

As I packed the lunch sack for my beloved this early morning, I thought about how simple it was to forgive once the initial offering was made. Watching the sunset as his truck drove away, I was reminded again of how simple life can really be. We humans tend to muck things up with so much extra window dressing. All we really need do is clear our minds of the nonsense and concentrate on what we really see, not just what we want to see.

Sometimes the view is cloudy and overcast. At other times, it is crystal clear.

Who approached who? Who held out their hand first in offering forgiveness? I really can't remember. It was if we did it simultaneously. I know that true forgiveness is worthless unless there is repentance offered up as well.

"Forgive me," it was said simply.

And we did.

It can be as simple as that.

GOOD-BYE

I don't do good-byes well.

Part of any journey to closure of something painful is the grieving process. We humans do love our rituals. I know all that in theory; practice is another thing altogether. Everything is different now, a new page in the evolution of our lives. I cannot say good-bye, so I won't. The best I can muster is, "See ya later."

It was hard to say good-bye to my father when he died, so I didn't.

There was a final viewing before he was cremated, and my siblings and I were given the option to say good-bye one more time.

I couldn't, so I didn't. I preferred to remember him the last time I was with him, making our dinner of mashed potatoes.

Our beloved pastor said his final Masses this weekend, and he greatly desired that all the staff be there. I made it to three of them; the last one I couldn't, so I didn't.

Each parish had its own unique way of saying good-bye with special prayers, songs, and blessings, all reflecting their own way of worshiping. His final homilies were about letting go of everything, for that is the way God wants it, and to focus on just the here and now. His own voice cracked every now and then; it belied his love for all of us, just as we love him.

"We let go of our children when they grow; we let go of our health when we grow old. Funerals are a way to practice our own release to enter into our final reward.

I don't know about you," he said to us, "but it seems the more I have to say good-bye, the easier it gets. Or maybe I'm just in denial."

I suspect it is a little of both.

"Whenever you start to miss how things used to be," he said, _nding what has been a heart-wrenching week, "just recall the spirit of what was."

I thought about the good-byes I didn't get to say. A girlfriend whom I had a disagreement with was suddenly stricken with a stroke and died days later. We never got the chance to speak again, and the best I could do was kiss her cheek, a sad gesture to a senseless ending.

Another girlfriend's farewell was intentional. Having been diagnosed with an inoperable tumor, she chose to forego any form of treatment, allowing herself to wither away and forbidding anyone to see her toward the end. Another kiss on a different cheek this time still warm but wet with tears.

Other good-byes have not resulted in death but in new life. A son's decision to move to another state brought back the memories of when he was young and still needed me to help steady his walk. Now strong and able to bound anywhere on his own, I vowed to remember the pastor's plea to "recall the spirit of what was."

We all smiled, tears rolling down our faces, as it was impossible to speak. Wet faces nodded in unison.

"I'm not going far, just across town, and I am sure we will see each other from time to time. But of course, it will be different."

Each congregation stood to applaud as he was finished, and I can only assume it was the same at the last Mass I didn't attend. I couldn't go, so I didn't. Struggling to keep my composure at the earlier Mass only confirmed what I knew my heart already knew.

Yes, everything is different now. I cannot say good-bye, so I won't. The best I can muster is, "See ya later."

May God hold you in the palm of his hand until we meet again.

FAMILY STORIES

MY MASHED POTATO DADDY

My father passed away on February 17, 2003. Rochester was in the midst of one of its worst snowstorms and the airports were shut down. I wasn't able to travel to Texas where my parents lived, and where my siblings had already gathered, until two days later. I never really got to say good-bye to him, but I realized a few days later that he had said good-bye to me five months earlier.

I wrote this column when I returned home, and it appeared in my first book, Rhythm and Rhymes of the Heart, 2003–2005. I find it hopelessly ironic that the love of my life was born one day later, February 18. I like to think my father would only want me to mourn him for one day and then get down to getting back to the life around me. I couldn't agree more. Goodnight, Daddy.

Since my father passed away two days ago, I have had time to think about my relationship with him over the past few years. It seems my dad and I never saw eye-to-eye on anything. We didn't have the same politics, we didn't agree on religion, and we certainly never talked about sex, except for him to tell me that I shouldn't have any. In fact, the only thing we agreed on was that we loved to laugh and tell jokes.

One thing I am sure of, however, is that he loved me and that I loved him. He was my daddy.

I am the oldest of six. When I was little, one of the ways my dad showed my mom how much he loved her was to let her sleep late on Saturday morning. He would make breakfast: eggs over easy, bacon and toast, with a side of hash browns with onions—I have never been able to duplicate the recipe. He could whip up French toast, sausages, and pancakes with the ease and finesse of any chef and not spill a drop or drop a dish.

My father had a lot of different interests, many diverse talents and hobbies. But to me, the thing he did best of all was make mashed potatoes. Creamy and light, whipped high with Land o' Lakes salted butter and whole milk, it was something we had every night with dinner, seven days a week. We never tired of it.

I realized in the plane over Chicago on the way to his funeral that was how my dad said good-bye to me, the last time I spent time alone with him and visited. My folks live in Texas.

Living in western New York and away from everyone, I didn't start traveling until very recently, as I didn't leave my own family much, and airline tickets were too expensive. Now that I'm older and my kids are grown, it has become a priority in my life to visit my siblings, who live all over this great country.

It was the last trip to Texas in September, where we all gathered to visit with each other. I was being chauffeured around to visit my brother's new house, when I thought about how my father's condition had deteriorated from when I had seen him two years earlier. He sat at the kitchen counter most of the day, watching TV, reading, or looking out the window. He sat there, alternating between his "breathing machine" (nebulizer) and smoking a cigarette. He rarely went out anymore and was resigned to spend his days in this peaceful prison he had created for himself. Dying from emphysema, he had accepted his fate, a slave to his addiction, and was content to live out his last days in this way. He would sit there, patiently waiting, until my mother came home from work. Then she would cook dinner, and they would share the rest of the evening together.

One morning, it was decided we were all going to my brother's house for dinner. As the day wore on, I started to feel a little queasy.

"Oops," they told me after a while. "Your stomach might be upset from the tap water; just drink the water out of this store-bought jug. Sorry! We forgot to tell you that might happen."

In all the excitement they forgot to mention it, something about too much chlorine in the water, but by that time it was too late. I spent most of the afternoon in the lavatory and was not feeling up to par for a dinner party. My stomach was raw, and all I wanted to do was lie on the couch and sip some hot tea.

I begged off. "I'll stay here with Dad," I volunteered. "We'll watch TV." As if this was a new activity for him. He just smiled.

After the 6:00 p.m. news was over, he looked down from his perch at the counter and said to me, "Hungry, kid?"

He called everyone "kid," even his own mother when she was alive.

"How 'bout some mashed potatoes?"

"Sure," I told him. "I'll make them, you stay put."

Having made them since I was a kid and watching his technique, I could prepare them with my eyes closed.

So I took out the potato peeler and began to peel what must have been my nine millionth potato, having carried on the tradition with my own family. Potatoes every night, except when we had pasta. I was an Irish girl who had married an Italian, after all.

I cut them in quarters the way I always had, but he pointed out to me they were too big.

"A little smaller," he directed from his command post.

"Measure the milk." I began to ready the hand mixer.

"Let me cut the butter," he added, "because you never put in enough."

Before I knew it, he was up off his stool and standing right next to me at the stove, his frustration getting the best of him.

"You can beat them with the mixer as I add the milk," he instructed.

So I stood there, standing at the stove like I had a hundred times before, and I waited as he poured the milk. As he stood next to me, I suddenly realized that my dad was now as short as me, having shrunk several inches over the years. He seemed to realize it too, as our eyes met in an instant, with the recognition of the loss of his stature.

"Hey, shorty." He smirked, the twinkle in his eyes still sharp. "Go sit down." So I did.

As he folded in the last chunks of butter into the pot, he absentmindedly hummed a tune that I couldn't place the name of but remembered from my childhood.

As is the tradition, he removed the beaters from the hand

mixer. In our family, the cook gets the first lick of mashed potatoes off the beaters, presumably to taste and see if it needs any more salt. But we all knew it was because they tasted so good and he couldn't resist.

He handed me the other beater, and we clicked them together like wine glasses at the conclusion of a toast announced at a fancy dinner. He looked at me and said, "You first."

So I did, and they were as I remembered. Delicious and pota-toey with just the right mix of butter and salt. Sitting at the kitchen counter, we ate the whole pot, just me and my dad. He hummed that song every now and then. After a while, I was humming along.

I've thought about that moment a lot since September, and the significance of it. The turn of events that led me to stay home with him that night. The song that I couldn't remember the name of but recognized so quickly. It wasn't until much later I realized the song he was humming was "Goodnight, Irene," but he always changed the name to "Eileen." He made the mashed potatoes because he knew that I loved them, and he knew that was all he had left to give me. I am so grateful to God for giving me that brief, silly moment with him. It was a wonderful gift I will remember always.

I know that he has shared himself with my sisters and brother in ways that are special just to them. I know that he said good-bye to my mother, the love of his life for fifty years, four months, and sixteen days, in a way that will warm her heart and keep her going. But I will be forever thankful that I had that night in the kitchen with my dad, eating mashed potatoes out of a pot and humming "Goodnight, Eileen."

Goodnight, Daddy. Rest in peace.

NAVY BOY

We drove together in silence, me at the wheel of my Ford Taurus and he looking out the window. He had repacked all his gear for his ten-day leave home to Rochester for the holidays. His life was in the trunk. He had just spent some precious time off the U.S.S. *Nimitz,* an aircraft carrier stationed in San Diego. He was halfway across the country and away from me and his three brothers and sister, from his dad in Chicago, and from his young daughter who lived with her grandma in Churchville; halfway through a six-year commitment to the service of a country he is so proud to serve.

We were headed for Buffalo, knowing his childhood would be left behind.

It was harder for him to leave this time.

He was home to see his friends, to visit his brothers and sister, and to see his daughter. I was part of the package, sandwiched in between a quick kiss and maybe a light breakfast or late-night supper. But that was all right with me, as long as I got to see him.

He spent his days sleeping late, after partying and movie going and looking at everyone's new digs. Most of the group he hung with now have apartments or have roommates in a house. They all have cars and jobs and/or go to grad school. They have Sony TVs, PlayStations, DVD players. Mostly, they all have debt. He has no debt, except for child support. He lives on a boat. They have freedom.

It was harder for him to leave this time.

I told him to hold on to some of the good times; when they were young, heck, we were all babies, and we all had a great time together while scraping a living and growing up together, day by day. This son is not my oldest, but he seemed to be the most mature. My husband used to laugh and say, "This kid was born forty years old." He seemed to know it too, and he accepted that role in the family.

I told him to remember the times he would just bust a gut laughing over some silly poopy joke he and his brothers had made up or sledding at Highland Park on that hill near the outdoor shell. I would take turns with all the kids, because "Mom might fall off." He still has that sense of humor, although the jokes are a little more vulgar than poopy jokes now but funny just the same. He is a sailor and feels the need to live up to being "salty."

My fondest, yet most heart-wrenching memory of him was a hot summer day when he was eight years old. I looked out the back window of our little house in the city and saw him and his friends sitting around a circle of rocks, holding sticks punctuated with cotton balls at the end. When I asked them what the heck were they doing now, he replied, "We're pretending we're at a campfire, Mom. You can't light a fire in the backyard in the city, right?" Then he turned back to the circle and continued leading them in singing "campfire" songs. I never told him that memory until now.

He smiled and realized the impact of all that had never been said between us before.

I didn't tell him about the memory of seeing the twin towers fall and wondering where he was on the ship, if the lunatics were going to start bombing ships too, like the U.S.S. *Cole.* I didn't tell him how I cried and thanked God on my knees when he finally called me with the usual, "Hey, turbo, how's it going?" I hold on to the campfire memory instead. It's how I can let him go.

But it was definitely harder for him to leave this time.

Not because he regretted his decision. Not because there might be a war. He's not a coward.

But because he now knows what he has signed up for is real. He is a defender of freedom.

He is my defender and that of his friends and brothers and sister. He is protecting the future for his daughter.

It was definitely harder for him to leave this time, but I am so proud that he did.

I gave my son back to Uncle Sam today. I hugged him tight when saying good-bye at the gate at the Buffalo Airport, and I didn't cry this time. Maybe because he held on to me a little bit longer before he let go. I kissed him and reminded him of this awesome job he has chosen, this path his life has taken. I reminded him that God is with him, always. We all were with him, always.

He is twenty-one years old. You can have him, Uncle Sam, for the time he will be gone. But I expect to get him back. He's my boy. My navy boy.

BINGO MARY

Bingo Mary stood four feet, eight inches tall, but she was a force to be reckoned with.

Whenever she spoke, it sounded as if she had just gotten off the boat the week before, and her Irish brogue was delivered with quick, staccato precision. Especially if she wanted to make a point.

Bingo Mary not only had several points a day to make, she was pretty prickly when expressing them. Don't bother to argue or have an opinion of your own, for you would lose no matter how hard you tried. But she did have a softer side that showed itself to me every now and then.

Before she lived with us, before my father gave her the moniker, Nana had her own house around the corner. My grandfather and her son, my favorite uncle, lived there too, but it was definitely Bingo Mary's house.

Reaching the age of wanderlust, I was too young yet to drive and too old to play with Barbie dolls. Saturday mornings were spent helping my mother clean or watching my sisters while she ran errands. My brother would be off with our father, doing "man" things, whatever that was. All I knew was that we girls weren't invited.

Needless to say, my freedom was severely limited back then, as I was needed to help my mother. My best friend, Ilene, lived up the street but would go to temple with her parents and not be around much on Saturdays.

So we fell into a routine, me, my mother, and Nana. I would help my mother in the morning and then could go to Nana's house to get a "treat."

Pepsi was the drink of choice in Nana's house, as it was in mine. But growing up in a house with a six-pack of Pepsi and as many kids, there wasn't an opportunity to have a can of soda to myself alone.

Also in short supply were potato chips and Juicy Fruit gum. I loved barbeque potato chips and could chew a packet of Juicy Fruit in an hour. I bought packet after packet so that I could make a paper chain from the wrappers, an exercise in patience and nimble fingers; I eventually created a snake-like chain that at its longest measured twenty-four inches long. That was a lot of gum.

It became a time that I looked forward to and a habit that lasted a long time. Clean in the morning; Nana's in the afternoon.

I would walk around the corner and wait for the trucks and cars to pass by before I could cross. This was important business, and I didn't want to get killed—not before I had my own Pepsi, that is.

It was always there, sitting on the kitchen table, alongside a bowl filled with barbeque potato chips. They were saltier then, in an age before sodium counts and blood pressure woes.

One summer day I was given a surprise gift. Suddenly and for no particular reason, there stood a blue leather case sitting on the kitchen table, off to the side of the bowl of chips and bottle of Pepsi.

I looked at her as if to say, "Who left this here?" but she smiled demurely as I put my hand on the leather case. Snugly packed inside was something that would change the route of my future. I reached around and found the zipper, pulling it all away around the case, setting free the instrument of my destiny.

I had always wanted to be a nurse when I grew up. It is all I ever wanted to do, and the desire to work toward that goal made its presence known in every moment of my young life.

My brother and his friends would play battle in the front yard, with wooden guns and hand grenades that resembled oranges. Invariably, someone would get wounded and they would yell, "Nurse!"

Out I would bound, as if waiting on the sidelines of a war, wet tissues in hand, and tend to the wound of the beleaguered soldier. Miraculously, he would be cured and get back into the war. I would smile and couldn't wait until I had real patients to work on, real miracles and victories all due to my nursing skill.

Those thoughts were gone forever as I opened up the door

to my real dream. It was a plastic, blue, portable typewriter, and I haven't stop typing since.

I often wonder on rainy days like today, as I sit and write another chapter to a story, why she felt it would benefit me to have such a contraption. Did she see something in me that my parents did not? Was she fulfilling something she never achieved, living through me?

Maybe she knew I would one day tell the story about her and my father, my mother and me.

Bingo Mary lives on in me, as all great characters live inside all of us. Refusing to fall to the wayside but bubbling up to the top of our consciousness, they are bits and pieces of who we are, where we came from, and what we can ultimately become.

Our only limits are our imagination.

YOU'RE WELCOME

The ride down was uneventful but full of promise.

We talked and laughed, remembering the first time we had made this trip. Her father and brothers were with us, taking her to a university one hundred miles away. It was close enough to come home on the weekends if she got homesick but far away enough to get her used to taking care of business on her own.

She hated it because it was a school I wanted her to attend, not the one she wanted to enroll in.

The second time we made a trip for school, we got halfway there and got caught in a snowstorm. We slept in the car for a little while and then turned back toward home.

This time we were prepared. She had money in her pocket that she had earned, had found the school she wanted in Manhattan, New York, and even found the funding to go with it.

The weather was perfect, made to order. Traveling at a speed of seventy miles per hour, we got there in time to check into an expensive hotel and enjoy the amenities.

We were alone this time, just her and me.

Finding the school was easy; parking was just as easy, albeit expensive, which was a pattern she was beginning to realize shortly after we arrived. We parked the car and walked to an Italian restaurant in Little Italy, feeling sophisticated and chic.

After eating a seventeen-dollar plate of spaghetti, we raised our wine glasses in a toast.

"I'm proud of you," I said with a smile

"I'm proud of me too," she said, draining her glass.

Living with four other young women, she has finally come into her own and will steer her own course to her destiny. I am not worried about her anymore.

Kissing her good-bye as I let her off in front of the apartment building one more time, she gave me a kiss on the cheek and a big hug that lasted longer than any other given before.

"Thank you," she said simply. "Thank you."

The moment every mother dreams of and hopes for with all heart.

Understanding.

You are welcome.

WHY DID YOU DO THAT?

I used to think it was the weather conditions that prompted the onslaught of memories I get sometimes. Most often they are of my dad and his influence in my life in ways I never realized.

On a cold wintry day, I would wrap myself in a quilt and look out at the snow-crusted lake, ice banks formed along the shoreline. I would drift back to when I was younger, much younger, and how much I hated the cold. Funny how it does not faze me in the least now, living in the frozen tundra of winter in upstate New York.

Rainy spring afternoons would often bring about thoughts of childhood and wondering how I survived half of what I attempted. My younger sister and I got lost in the woods once, even though it was near my house. Being the oldest, I decided my sister and several of my visiting cousins were going to go on a nature walk. The relatives were in town from New York City, and I was anxious to show off my nature skills. I was eight years old, and my cousins ranged from five, six, and seven. There were six of us.

I figured that I would just leave signs at the turn of every tree; a particular rock or a bush would be my markers. The only thing nature girl didn't realize is that when returning back from trekking through the woodlands, all the aforementioned markers looked the same.

I knew that we were lost, but somehow it didn't seem to bother me. I knew someone would find me, and sure enough, I heard my father's voice loud and clear, calling for me through the thick underbrush and fallen pines.

Walking back toward the house, he suddenly stopped and asked me his patented question to make me realize I had taken a wrong turn.

"Why did you do that?" my dad asked simply, as if there was

some great truth pulling at me that had to be answered that day. But he knew the answer.

"I dunno," I answered just as simply. "I just felt like walking."

This morning's beautiful sunrise brought forth another memory.

With my three-year-old son in tow and money in my pocket, I jumped in a van with a friend, and we drove to Phoenix, Arizona. Had one of my children done this today, I would have surely killed them, but I paid no mind as to what my parents might be thinking or feeling. I was full of myself, the wanderlust, longing for adventure.

I found work in a hospital and made lots of friends. The sunrises were spectacular, but I knew that this was not the place for me. I knew I was lost, but it didn't seem to bother me.

When I got off the bus at the station many months later, tired but happy to be home, my father came to retrieve us, not too gently this time.

"Why did you do *that?*" my father asked once again, looking for some clue as to why I thought the way I did.

"I dunno," I replied again. "I just felt like driving."

Of all the times I needed my father, I thought he wasn't there. Growing older I realized how much he said without saying a word, just asking a question now and then. He was always there, whether I wanted him to be or not. He saw some of me in himself, I suspect, and quietly bragged to anyone who would listen how his oldest daughter had chutzpah and wasn't afraid of anything. Maybe it was because I was too naïve to be afraid; maybe I was just stupid. My father gave praise sparingly, so I reveled in whatever he had to offer.

His birthday is July 9, and he will have been gone four years this coming February. I miss him more than I thought I ever would.

As I sit out on the deck and watch the sun rise high in the sky, I realize it has nothing to do with the weather conditions at all. He is sitting next to me, watching me and still trying to figure out what makes me tick. My memories are of him and my mother, my siblings, and my cousins, the ones I almost lost in the woods so many years ago.

The cell phone purred quietly next to my chair, and I picked it up to hear the voice of my son, all grown up now, the one who had gotten in a van and drove to Colorado.

"Why did you do that?" I asked him softly, but I already knew the answer.

I swear I could feel my father sitting next to me, smiling.

PINEAPPLE UPSIDE-DOWN CAKE

The kids were over for dinner last night, and even though they are no longer children, I like to put together a menu that is reminiscent of when they were.

The one serving our country is back on dry land after six years and no worse for wear from the experience. He is older, wiser, and more mature. A natural progression, of course, but it is still odd to see him as a man.

Standing next to him at the front door was his best friend and my seventh child, Jon. They have been friends since kindergarten, and it is my deepest joy that they have remained friends all these years. I believe the art of friendship is the biggest gift you can pass on to your children.

Dinner was meatloaf and an old favorite for dessert: pineapple upside-down cake.

It immediately brought a smile to his face when I brought it into the dining room, steaming hot and bubbling. For this was his first attempt at cooking while in first grade, a project all students were asked to do.

"Bake something with your parents and bring it to school!" the flyer said.

"I want to make a pineapple upside-down cake!" he announced proudly. "Can we?"

I looked at him and smiled, even though I didn't have a clue back then as how to assemble one.

Thank goodness for the *Betty Crocker Cookbook* I had received when I was first married at twenty-one years old. It had followed me from house to house and had served me well. I learned how to make chicken pot pies and far too many variations of meatloaf than I cared to admit, but it was a great source of information. It taught me how to get out of more scrapes in the kitchen than I could have imagined.

"Sure," I answered happily as I reached for the good book. "Let's find a recipe."

Needless to say, the pineapple upside-down cake was a success, and he talked about it for days on end until even his baby sister couldn't stand it any longer.

"Why did you want to make that cake, anyway?" she asked, exasperated. "What's so special about that cake?"

She had asked the question I had been rolling around in the back of my mind since he had asked for it. Since I had never made it before, I wondered why he was even interested in it.

Looking at me with the pride I still see in his eyes to this day, he answered. I will never forget the dedication and unabashed affection in his voice as he told me simply and without embarrassment.

"It's my best friend Jon's favorite cake," he said joyfully, and then he turned to run into the living room. The *Transformers* were on TV, one of his favorite shows.

He and Jon are friends for life. After finishing up his six-year tour of duty in the navy, he knew there was a room waiting for him at Jon's house until he was ready to find his own place. It had never been discussed between them; it was just a fact of life. They were the fortunate ones, learning at such an early age how important friendship can be.

The memory of that day has been tucked away in my mind and wasn't brought back out until I laid the cake in front of him again last night after dinner. We smiled, as no words were needed. I cut the cake in giant squares to pass along with vanilla ice cream. They sat and ate, good-natured ribbing and affection between them, as only men can do.

For we know that good friends are forever, no matter what.

JOKES AND NUMBERS

I have always been a performer in one fashion or another. Whether it be from the pulpit or at a seminar, I have never been afraid to speak in public.

Truth is, I love the spotlight. I am the perennial ham, and my friends forgive me for it. I love a good laugh, and when the joke is on me, I laugh the loudest.

Of course, there is a time and a place for everything. But that didn't stop me from being the class clown, the jokester, or being "just plain silly" as my father would say.

Hogging the spotlight sometimes interfered with my school-work, and that was not a good thing. Auditions and play rehearsals always seemed to get in the way of homework. To be precise, my math studies.

Multiplication tables, in particular.

My father was determined I would learn them. He bought flash cards, and we would spend hours trying to get those sequences into my head.

It was not very practical and frustrating for all involved. My sisters and brother would go running for cover every time they saw the box of cardboard squares come out of the dining room dresser drawer.

We discovered that I am not a visual person; I learn better by rote. The only way I could learn them was to repeat them, over and over, much like learning the lines in a play.

Or a comedy routine.

Sitting at the dinner table, I would have a mouthful of mashed potatoes when my father would yell out, "Six times four!" He was relentless, and he went through every table from one through twelve until I was correct. My sisters told me years later they learned them vicariously through me.

"Twenty-four!" Yes! Got it right, that way I knew I would only have about ten more outbursts during the night. He would be in the middle of a conversation with my mother and then suddenly turn toward me and yell, "Seven times five!"

While talking on the phone with my best friend, Ilene, I would get pulled aside and his big smiling face would assault me, a burning cigarette stick stuck in the side of his mouth like a maniacal Popeye.

"What's two times nine?" And he wouldn't let me finish the conversation until I answered.

"Eighteen." Then I returned my attention to the task at hand, listening to the latest lament about a boy, wondering if her father was as goofy. I already knew the answer. Probably not.

I would be brushing my teeth before bed when suddenly he would stick his head in the bathroom. "Nine times nine!"

"Eighty-one," I answered as I spit a mouthful of toothpaste into the sink.

It's a great memory.

My beloved writes most of his jokes; although I am able to get in a few laughs here and there, he orchestrates the ebb and flow of the words, creates the mood and the comeback lines for me. I am the proverbial straight man and zig to his every zag.

We are a good team.

Just like my multiplication tables.

A WORD ABOUT SONS

A few important words about having sons.

God, in his infinite wisdom, saw fit to bless me with three of them, although I didn't realize they were a blessing at the time because they kept on coming one right after the other. I thought I was prepared. I found out in a hurry that nothing prepares you for raising a son.

My boys were like little men in their cotton pajamas. I always had to cut the feet off the one-piece heavy winter pajamas because their feet would sweat so badly. The smell was enough to make you keel over, and this was *after* they were potty trained. How the heck can a two-year-old get athlete's foot? I was constantly bathing them and sprinkling Gold Bond Power down their pant legs before they put them on. I used so much powder they would leave a trail of smoke behind them. So finally, I would have to get out the scissors.

Potty training is really different when dealing with a boy versus instructing a girl about the art of "going potty." With a girl you can show her how you sit down, position yourself, and do your business. With a boy … well … you need a daddy to show him.

One son was toothless 'til he was almost three years old; another had a full set of choppers when he was eleven months old. Two were outgoing; one was so shy he would dive under the couch anytime anyone came to the door. They were so different from each other, but you knew they were brothers.

I sent them all to college prep high schools with the expectation I would be producing a lawyer, a doctor, and an architect.

They all planned to be ghostbusters. Or ninjas.

For a while I thought they were all going to grow up to be plumbers because they loved to go to the hardware store. One day they surmised they were in some kind of birthing room for plungers because the smaller ones were laid out in a section on the floor, waiting to be put up for display. One of them came running down the aisle screaming, "Look at all these baby plungers, Ma. Isn't it *great?*" It was bathroom heaven, and they were ecstatic. Seeing the toilets was the closest thing to nirvana. I still haven't figured that one out.

There was also the time they thought they were going to be garbage men. But when they realized they had to get out of the truck and not just drive it, it lost its appeal. As they got older, they were always concocting some kind of backyard mud, water, and leaves soup, or mud pie sandwiches, or mud and grass meatballs. Their baby sister was the willing guinea pig, to "pretend taste" their culinary creations. At least I hope it was pretend taste. Ironically, even with a chef in the family, none of them are interested in cooking for a living. They were war heroes, using sticks as rifles when I went through my period of "no guns." They would make up weapons anyway. They traveled through the desert on their bellies rescuing each other from their enemies. It is the nature of man. No one ever died in their wars, and someone was always rescued before dinner.

They step to their own drummer, and I'm grateful they let me sit in on the dance. They are artists in their souls. They are painters, writers, singers, and musicians. They are who they are going to be. I had to embrace the reality of what that really meant before anyone could move forward. They are good at what they do, and they are happy. They are strong and healthy, confident and clear in what they want.

I'm not saying there haven't been bumps along the way. The great hodge-podge that came out of this family soup is flavored with tattoo art, piercings, and babies born too soon. There have been late-night calls for pickup because they couldn't drive. Thanks be to God they knew to call. They called me or had one of their friends call me. It didn't happen often, but it was a scary time. I didn't know where my little boys were, and I didn't know *who* they were. But I was trying to force square pegs into round holes. They just weren't going to fit.

Not one of them finished college, and for a long time I had a really hard time with that. I had always said that I wanted to raise interesting children. When I did, I was mad at them. I wanted them to be interesting in *my* way. But who else got what I did? I have received songs for Christmas, cartoon drawings on my birthday, and essays of love and appreciation out of the blue.

So, now when I look back, I know I have produced great men. I was the one with the problem. Not them.

I hope that I have raised them to someday be great husbands. They know how to treat women, and they take care of their mother. They also take care of each other and their sisters. They will make great fathers. No one could ask for more.

My sons. I love them; I am very proud. God, in his infinite wisdom, saw fit to bless me with three of them. I will be forever grateful.

I'LL GET THERE. WHAT'S THE RUSH?

"Come on! Let's go! We'll be late!"

Such were the words invariably yelled toward my mother's direction, every time we had to go shopping for school clothes, or any kind of shopping for anything, for that matter.

Always in a hurry; always yelling; always frustrated. Anyone who is a parent knows the worst thing to come across during the day is a frustrated teenage girl.

It's a wonder I didn't end up with an ulcer or a nervous breakdown, or give one to anyone else.

It was as if there was an internal clock ticking the minutes away in my mind. I was forever planning and scheduling. Every minute that got away was another minute wasted.

"Will you slow down?" she would reply calmly.

"What is the hurry? The clothes/makeup/jewelry will still be there when we get there," she'd say, smiling, substituting whatever material object I just *had* to have at that moment.

Slowly and deliberately she would meander down to the kitchen. Standing at the stove she would make herself her morning tea while the face of her seething daughter twitched and watched, trying to sit quietly. Every cell in my body exploded with impatience.

I was always racing, my heart pounding with excitement at the thought of having something to do and somewhere to go.

If you wanted something done quickly, give it to me. I was a voracious reader, and this was light years before the Internet. If you needed something researched, give it to me and I would find it quickly.

If you wanted something organized, however, give it to someone else. *That* took too much time.

As the years went by and children became part of the landscape, I began to notice something. I was missing out on the best part of having children—watching them grow.

It is a slow process that pays no mind to schedules, routines, or deadlines and is along the same lines as watching paint dry and pots boil. Luckily, I raised up my head and took a look back.

I realized I had to stop moving so quickly and let them catch up with me.

Gone were the lists of people to visit, places to go, tasks to accomplish. The floor wasn't washed every other day, and the furniture became so dusty you could write your request for dinner across the dining room buffet.

I began telling them made-up stories, and each adventure added another character as the years went by, as another child entered the family.

It was the best time of my life, and I shake my head from side to side when I think of how I very nearly missed it all.

"Come on, Mom! Let's go! We'll be late!" my teenage daughter yelled to me on an afternoon, not much different from this one. She had been in the car with it running in the driveway, alerting me to the time.

"I'm coming," I answered softly, smiling as I shut off the computer.

"The makeup/jewelry/clothes will still be there when we get there. What's your hurry?"

I looked around at my sparkling kitchen, for now I have more time to do less. I take a picture in my mind of the matching dishcloths and placemats so part of the landscape now. The refrigerator boasts of colorful pictures drawn by the hands of my loving grandchildren.

"I'm coming," I repeated with just a wisp of sadness, closing the front door behind me. "What's your hurry?"

WESLEY

The firstborn has the dubious distinction of being the test case, the one mothers practice on.

Mothers always learn what *not* to do with the first child from their womb, the lucky son or daughter who either gets to do everything or is sheltered from all that is out there in the world. They learn how to establish routines, how to cook for them, what is acceptable behavior, and what is not. How much of the proverbial leash to hold close or how much slack to let go of so that they can run freely, or at least let them think they are.

Mothers also have the responsibility of making sure they complete this on-the-job training before the next child shows up. Sometimes there is a sizeable window of time; other times the window is only open a crack before the next sibling arrives.

I consider my situation unique, since I tend to think I have two oldest sons. The first time I was very young and did not prepare for his arrival. The other oldest son would come six years later, after I had remarried and had forgotten most of the training from the seminar that was my Wesley.

For it is upon Wesley that I cut my teeth in the knowledge of mothering. Barely twenty-one years old, I had run away from home to elope with my high school sweetheart, also named Wesley. Nice girls didn't move away from their parents' houses until they were married. Being that I was a nice Catholic girl who longed for independence from my parents, I got married.

A real oxymoron if you ask me.

"Why don't we drive down to Maryland and elope?" he asked me one summer afternoon. "It will be fun." An adventure was what I was looking for. Having just completed a semester of community college, I wanted to go away somewhere.

I should have just gone on vacation.

Ten months to the day we were married, I gave birth to my son, the one who came with me on the first leg of my journey toward discovery of who I was, not to be completed until some twenty-five years later. He was the one who sat on the bus with me as we traveled cross-county back to the home of my parents, the home I had tried so desperately to escape.

We both learned together what it takes to survive in this world. His journey took him a different direction than mine, sometimes butting heads with what he was taught, his steely blue eyes always questioning everything and accepting nothing. He became so foreign to me, getting tattoos and piercings, adorning the once pristine body I had given him. Never one to be self-destructive, drugs and booze didn't appeal to him; his only distractions were music and girls.

His journey has taken him from New York to Colorado, to Arizona and Utah, and back to New York again. He has worked odd jobs and held some fairly odd positions. He was always a likeable person, with personality and charm opening many doors I would have not dared walked through. He had a calmness about him sometimes mistaken for maturity.

He was the first to say, "It's okay, Mom. Just be happy," when I announced I was getting divorced again. He became the role model for my other children, the second wind at an attempt of raising a family. He showed them it's okay to come from a "broken home," that your parents aren't losers or failures as people.

At my fiftieth surprise birthday party this past week, he surprised me with a gift that was more poignant than anyone other than he and I could fathom.

My column describing the early years of my life and the purple suitcase that accompanied us became quite prophetic. When I reread it now, I am stunned at the turn of events my life has taken since that date, the chance that I took in traveling to my dearly beloved, one with whom I will be with forever.

"For your new life, Mom," he said, his eyes shiny and bright as the one I love stood beside me to accept it.

The gift?

A suitcase.

My purple suitcase will become a planter in a far-off corner of the yard of my home on the Great Lake, a wonderful reminder of my old life when it was just me and the boy, a man now winking at thirty, a prophetic tool that led me to the one true love of my life, and who has my children's blessing.

For although he has trained me in the art of mothering, I wish that I could have done better by him and that life didn't have to be as hard as it was when he was younger.

His birthday is next month, and I wish nothing but happiness and joy. I am proud of him and hope he realizes how much I love him.

My gift to him will not be a suitcase but a picture frame. It will hold a photograph of not only him and me but of my other children, of my dearest love, and of course, Riley.

My family.

THE OSCAR GOES TO...

I never thought I'd end up here.

I was supposed to be living in New York City by now, as a famous comedic actress on Broadway. I was supposed to have received numerous Tony Awards for my stellar performances in various musicals as a singer and dancer and accolades for the countless Neil Simon plays written just for me.

Everybody said I was supposed to be a star. All my teachers, my friends, my drama coach. I could cry on cue, deliver a line without mistake, and hit my mark every time. Directors were amazed at the volume of speech coming from this little body. I could belt out a song and not break a sweat. I learned how to pose and how to strut. If I didn't make it on Broadway, it was a no-brainer that I could be a Rockette at Radio City Music Hall. Amateur photographers would take my pictures for college portfolios, saying I could use them for my casting call rounds. I did summer stock productions from 1972–1974. I did go for a casting call once, in 1973.

Then I got married.

Dreams of youth have a way of crashing down around you. Reality sets in. I got pregnant shortly after the marriage. We were both children, raising a child. He was a student, and I worked in a psychiatric hospital. My stellar performances were limited to sad, mentally ill women and a two-month-old. Tough crowd.

As time went on and I became a single mother, I never gave up the dream of becoming a star. But motherhood has a way of knocking everything out of your knapsack and replacing it with baby bottles, toys, and teething rings. My casting bag became a baby bag. I realized I had this little life I was responsible for, and I had to make a choice. It was getting crowded in my knapsack.

I never looked back. I am happy with the choice I made, that of being a mom. I was a star to five more children as the years went by. My talent now lies within them. They are writers, singers, song-writers, photographers, musicians, artists, and comedians.

They are my greatest achievements, the result of stellar performances of determination, education, and compassion. They are my Tonys, my Oscars, my Emmys. Their pictures decorate every wall of my house, every corner of my office. Because I chose them over myself, I will forever have them as statues on my mantle. They have done me proud, and my ambitions and dreams will live on in them.

I never thought I'd end up here. But I am so glad I did.

TWENTY-FIVE WATCHES

Several years ago, my beloved's stepmother passed away and left behind an unusual gift. A cache of everything I had ever wanted in the way of jewelry. I was the recipient of the remnants of an obsession, a collection of earrings, rings, necklaces, bracelets, and watches, most of it costume jewelry.

"Here, do you want this?" her daughter had asked me, tired from sorting and packing. We were standing in her mother's former bedroom, now a storage space for all she had collected. One wall was stacked from floor to ceiling full of dolls, collectable and rare, sleeping safely within their boxes. The opposite wall held up other boxes filled with shoes, bags, and various toiletries. I don't think she ever opened any of them. I think they were most likely bought during lonely nights alone watching the home shopping networks. She had also fulfilled her quota of kitchen appliances, baskets, and wigs, all which had already been divided up between the other women relatives. I had only met her three years earlier and didn't spend much time with her. I was the last to know her, the last to get there, and the last to say good-bye.

"So do you want them?" she asked me again, her voice tired but not impatient. She knew what this all looked like to those who really didn't know her mother. She wanted to put it all to rest, along with the memories and the clutter. Standing to face me, she handed me two large boxes, each containing plastic bags sorted with the various pieces: rings in one bag, necklaces in another, etc. She held them out to me, arms stretched taut so that I could see her triceps. There was a lot of heavy metal there, and she wasn't going to take no for an answer. For someone who had one good watch, five rings, and a couple of stainless steel earrings, this was the mother lode.

"I will be happy to take it, but don't you want some of it?" I asked as she transferred the weight of the boxes to me.

"This junk?" She laughed. "No, you can have it, and if you find there's really nothing you want, feel free to throw it away." Content the responsibility was now mine, she moved quickly on to the next project.

"Hey!" she yelled toward the room where she was heading. "Who wants these CDs?"

The next few weeks were spent uncovering my surprise treasures, quickly realizing there were so many pieces I had to purchase a jewelry armoire to store them. Even more surprising was the possibility that some of the rings (fifty-five in all) might have real gems in them, not just glass stones. Much to my husband's chagrin, I decided not to learn the value of them; I was happier thinking they were all real diamonds and gemstones.

Taking them to a jeweler I trusted would be time consuming and take the mystery out of the whole experience. No, I was better off not knowing because had I known the market value, I would not have worn them.

Their value to me was priceless, appraised or not. Happily, I did keep some of the watches out of the total sixty-nine I counted. Some were plastic and others were the result of the purchase of many drive-thru dinners when she didn't feel like cooking.

None of them worked. I kept twenty-five of the watches, to be exact. Some were very pretty, more ornamental than functional, and I thought perhaps I would just wear them as bracelets and not be concerned about whether they kept the correct time. After all, I had gotten this far without ever really knowing what the hour was, and I never seemed to be late for anything.

With no sounds of *tick-tick-tick* in the background of my mind, I was soon to learn a lot of people *do* want to know what time it is, and I had to keep explaining why the watch I was wearing was really a bracelet. I realized I was doing her a disservice by not wearing them and sharing them with the rest of the world. What would be the harm? All they needed was batteries and a cleaning. I would think of her every time I strapped one on.

What better tribute to her than that?

"Wow," said the man behind the counter. "Looks like you've

got a lot of time on your hands." We both laughed as I handed him the plastic baggie full of timepieces.

Time is all we really have, and we best not waste it. If I can carve out enough to glance at my wrist now and then, I will consider it a blessing. She did.

SUPER BOWL, STEAK, AND
A BAKED POTATO

Now that the Giants have won the Super Bowl, it is time to move on to other things of importance, such as Valentine's Day, Fat Tuesday, and Presidents Day Sales!

As I sat and munched my pizza with my beloved, the dogs at our feet as we cheered on our team, I was reminded of another time and place where the food was much more delectable and the memories were just as sweet.

I was never a football fan; my interest was more toward baseball and hockey.

But football was the rule of the house when the kids were young. Football season was a time where no one got to watch cartoons, nobody could come over to play; football was on.

Sundays were spent going to church and then home to either play catch in the backyard, rake some leaves, or shovel some snow, whatever the season brought.

But Super Bowl Sunday was different.

The Super Bowl was a party, and even though there was little money, I always splurged for the Super Bowl.

The menu for those late afternoon games was filled with delicacies, like filet mignon steak, a baked potato, and creamed corn.

But memorable for all for them was that they got to eat on the floor in the living room, in front of the TV.

It was something so foreign to them; it was my cardinal rule that no one ate in front of the TV, and there certainly was no food allowed in the living room.

It started when they could barely chew the steaks themselves. What a great surprise, they were eating in the living room! It was the most exciting thing they had ever heard of, and on the floor yet! A blanket lay on the floor like a picnic; it became a tradition they looked forward to every year.

They are all grown up and on their own now; I thought about that today as I sat watching the ice melt on the lake. I wondered if they remembered.

They did. Many different years brought many wonderful surprises.

The son in the navy called from the ship, far away from us and always in danger.

"Got your steak, Ma?" said the voice on the other line, and I almost burst into tears.

The son in Colorado called from his townhouse.

"Eatin' some baked potato today, Ma. How about you?"

The son and daughter who lived in the city back then were partying, but they made time to call and ask the ultimate question. Even now they call to see how I am doing and if I've carried the tradition on with my husband.

Just like back then.

I can still picture in my mind's eye the look on their faces that first Super Bowl afternoon.

Spread in a circle on the floor, they held their dishes up as I handed out the slivers of filet mignon, plopped a small baked potato wrapped in tin foil on their plate, and let them scoop their own creamed corn onto their dish.

"Are we rich, Mom?" my warrior daughter asked with all the awe of Cinderella being told she was really a princess.

I looked around at the shiny faces, and my heart was filled with love.

This was one of those moments you keep close to you for when you need them. It's what helps you get through the night when all is confused and keeps you from killing them when they try to push their limits.

"Yeah, Ma, are we rich?" navy boy asked.

I looked at them in their hand-me-down jeans and flannel shirts, worn thin in the arms but still wearable.

My quiet son was smiling softly as he looked at the design of the tinfoil and wondered if he could draw that.

The baby sat wide-eyed in her pink sweat suit with a Care Bear appliqué on the front, an outfit I had picked up at a garage sale for fifty cents.

"Today we are," I said as I turned my face so they didn't see the tears.

Today we are.

I hope you celebrated your own tradition on Super Bowl Sunday—and if you didn't, it's time to make some.

Make your own traditions, for they will remember them when they need them.

Have a steak and a baked potato on me.

Eat in the living room on the floor.

Happy Super Bowl!

RIGATONI DAY

"Where would you like to go for lunch?" I asked my son this snowy winter day. He had a day off and wanted to spend some precious time left to just hang out with me.

"You pick, but I'm buying," he answered with a big smile. He'd been waiting to treat me for quite a while. Now that he could, he would take advantage of the situation.

We drove to an old Italian restaurant in the city where I used to take all of my kids for dinner. Nothing special, it was housed in an old building, the inhabitants of the kitchen living upstairs for more than thirty years.

It reminded me of the small Italian eateries on the streets of Philadelphia and New York City, with just as much ambiance. Everywhere you looked there could have been a wise guy, as well as a politician. Many deals were made at those small round tables, for every conversation was within earshot of another.

The neighborhood was old and run down, the victim of the loss of businesses and plants that had shut down and moved farther south or to Mexico. Revitalization of the area was promised more than once, and the politicians who graced the tables never thought twice about saying this place was a vital part of the city and should be saved. Twenty years later, the building still stands none the worse for wear, revitalization not withstanding.

The little restaurant has been cooking the same simple food for more than fifty years, so we didn't need a menu to order. Only certain things were served on certain days, with no deviation for any reason. It worked. It was Thursday, rigatoni day.

The cold air swooshing behind us as we walked to the counter, the memories flooded back at the sight of the wooden bar and glass mirror on the wall behind it. Like a scene out of every *Godfather* movie, there were men sitting at the bar, eating their tripe and salad, staples of every good Italian diet. Soup and salad were also part of the package. It was good, hearty food, and the helpings were generous in size and flavor. The aromas were amazing, and the smell of the red sauce permeated the walls.

"Rigs with a meatball, salad, and a glass of wine, Joe." And the man who stood before me as I pointed to my table smiled.

"How ya been?" he said and gave me a bear hug. Twice my size, he was tall and dark, a slowly receding hairline the only telltale sign of his aging. His muscular arms held tight the pad of paper and short stub of a pencil, and his mouth opened wide at the sight of my son. He was used to seeing me now without the man who used to walk behind the caravan of kids.

"Is this the boy?" he asked, incredulous, and we all smiled, grateful he was home after serving his six-year commitment to the U.S. Navy. Wars leave scars, memories, and grateful prayers upon everyone's heart.

Witnessing the scene between us was a man who sat in the corner table by himself. He introduced himself to us, and talk quickly turned to Korea and Iraq, then and now. He showed us the watch he bought in an old store in 1945 and how he only had to wind it once a day. He wouldn't trade it for any of the new models that did not need winding.

We talked about other restaurants and compared our notes of favorites, traded gossip about who was cooking where, who opened their own place or who closed because they were tired.

As talk progressed to kids and families, I learned he was the man who first laid the front lawn of my beloved's uncle's house, sometime in the 1950s. We laughed and banged the table as we traded names of recognition, and phrases like, "Do you know?" and "Where is he now?" and "When did she die?" flew back and forth between the spaces.

As my son paid for the bill, a fraction of what would have been charged had we gone to another eatery, my mind drifted back to when my kids were younger and we sat around the bigger round tables saved for families. It was now occupied by old Italian men (very few women) and not the white collar executives who ran there between meetings. I wondered where this place would be in ten years.

If the tables could talk, I know there would be quite some stories to share. I felt lucky to have been part of the journey, to have the memory of this place tucked behind my ear like a flower off the stem.

"See you next time!" the old man/new friend said as we opened the door, cold air greeting us once again.

See you on Rigatoni Day.

NAIL POLISH

When my youngest daughter was ten years old, she would ask me to paint her nails with nail polish. This was quite an occasion, as she was very much the tomboy for many years. Having three older brothers will do that to you, I guess. It always made her want to keep up with them, if not outdo them completely.

So when she came to me with the request, I would immediately put down what I was doing, whether it be folding laundry or talking on the phone, making dinner or paying bills. I would delight in doing this motherly activity with her, her tiny little nail beds shiny with color when we were done. It was something we could do together, a moment in time where she would let me fuss over her and wallow in being feminine. The colors were invariably blue or violet, although I always tried to get her to opt for the traditional pink or light tan, silvery white or sparkly clear.

Silly me. I should have accepted way back then that my daughter was not cut from any traditional cloth and would beg for bright red. The dark black polish of her "goth" phase would not arrive until several years later. We would compromise and settle on a dark, creamy magenta or the blue and violet. As she got older, *The Rocky Horror Picture Show* was one of her favorite movies. She got me to go with her to a performance one Halloween when she was eighteen, dressed up as a character and participating in the show within the show in the theatre. It was great fun and we laughed ourselves silly, a great memory we pull out now and then, painting our nails dark and wearing dark lipstick.

Chemotherapy has a way of making time stand still. When she was halfway through her treatment phase, the telltale signs of the illness were evident when she looked in the mirror. She was never one to feel sorry for herself, and her sadness only showed itself sporadically in bursts of frustration or impatience. Most of the time she would slap on a wig, pencil in eyebrows, and paste on some eyelashes. She had no shortage of dates, the phone ringing off the hook after dancing with friends over the weekend. She knew the cosmetics were only window dressing to the gift she is inside, the real reason they called her. They called her because she is fun, she is sweet, and she is confident. This damn cancer is just a pain in the neck, and *"Let's get over it, okay?"* I was, and am to this day, awed by her strength and determination.

But there were days when she was fearful, as one so young would normally feel. She lay in a lounge chair, the tubes inserted into the implant surgically inserted in her chest shortly after the diagnosis. First, blood was drawn to check her white cell count. "Pray to the vein goddess, Venus Arterioles." She laughed, to make sure everything was going according to schedule. It was. Saline was injected to clean the vein and pave the way for the drugs to continue the war against this evil that has invaded her body. I sat beside her the five hours it took for her to receive it all, my emotions doing battle in my own mind.

"I hate this chemo," she said abruptly one morning after they had just drawn blood. "I hate the smell; I hate how it tastes; I hate it all. I can see why people just say screw it and let themselves die."

I looked at my brave tough one, the one voted "Most Outspoken" in high school. I grabbed her hand and kissed it, the brown nail polish she had applied the day before glistening in the sterile white room, a room in the hospital where she was hooked up once a month for the cocktail, a combination of four drugs that was killing the cancer that had disturbed her otherwise perfect body. The drugs were working; the tumors were eventually killed off. They are now just a bad memory of a battle won, the conquering hero of the villain known as Hodgkin's lymphoma. She and I both know she has dodged a very big bullet. Things could have been so much worse. But it didn't make things any easier.

I held her hand that day and said to her matter-of-factly, "Look at it this way. Think of this chemo as nail polish remover and the nail polish the cancer. Little by little, layer by layer, the polish will be wiped away, until the clean nail beds are visible once again."

Rolling her eyes, she mocked me. "You and your stupid analogies." She smirked at me. "Why do you do that?" She laughed, knowing full well the answer.

She was beginning to get sleepy, her pupils widening from the dose of Marinol, a derivative of marijuana that helped with nausea. I would grow acres of it just for her if I could.

"I do it so you have a visual to work with, to make you feel better and to help you cope," I answered nonchalantly. "And I do it to make me feel better too," I added sheepishly.

She smiled again and rolled on her side in the chair, the toxins flowing through her bloodstream beginning to take its effect.

"You are such a sap." She laughed softly, drifting off to sleep.

"The sappiest." I giggled, turning my head so she wouldn't see the tears.

I just returned from a weekend in New York City, where she now lives and works. Now twenty-five years old, she has met a nice guy and will most likely begin a new adventure with him. She is happy and healthy and knows time is never to be wasted.

My Thanksgiving prayers have become and always will be a simple one to the Almighty.

Thank you.

.

NEW YORK NANA

I am in Denver this week, staying with my oldest son and his fiancée, a beautiful girl who has a daughter named Alyssa who is four years old today.

Pretty as a little doll with long blonde hair, she is polite and very self-assured for such a young age. I was amazed at her sense of confidence and intelligence, talking to me and telling me about her cats. She is sitting on my lap as I write this column, referring to me as her "New York Nana" and how glad she is to see me.

Also visiting this week is my son's father, my first husband and high school sweetheart.

We laughed as we all had dinner at our son's restaurant and spent some time catching up and talking about high school and what we've been doing the last thirty years. Who needed a class reunion when he could tell me everything I wanted to know about who did what and where they were?

It was a relaxing and fun time, and I sat next to him as our son snapped a picture of us together. I realized that he never had a picture of his parents standing in one place at the same time, for the marriage was over before it begun. We were divorced by the time he was six months old, each of us marrying other spouses who loved him and called him their own. I am sure the wedding photographs will be one for the books.

Walking to the car after a great dinner, we stopped to look at each other for just a moment. I could tell by his face he wanted to say something, and I nodded in agreement.

"I wouldn't have changed a thing," I said simply.

"What was meant to be was meant to be." And he gave me a big hug.

Bitterness is an unwelcome visitor who doesn't stay at my house very long.

"Let's go, New York Nana!" chirped the little voice behind me. "Time to go home."

We smiled as we each went to our cars, remembering the freshness and innocence of youth, the excitement of young love, and the realization that we had forgiven each other many times over.

We will spend the rest of our days as friends

Perhaps one day we will sit in a restaurant and talk about our granddaughter who is getting married, snapping a picture of us and boasting about her grandparents, as well as Grandpa Steve. The past is always remembered with fondness, and hard times fade away like voices on the wind. Everything is how it should be. For that I am thankful.

MY MOTHER'S TRIP TO VENUS

It was a phone call I hoped I would never receive.

My father passed away six years ago on a cold February morning, and I had gotten the call from my sister-in-law.

"Honey," she said, "I have bad news. Your daddy's gone."

It was somewhat of a shock, but not really. My brother and his wife lived in a small town outside Houston, on the other side of Sugarland, where my parents lived. Knowing my mother was now going to be living by herself, my sisters and I reasoned she would live as independently as she wanted. The last few years of my parents' time together were spent mostly of her tending to her ceramic business in the daytime and tending to my father in the evening. Her customers would wait patiently by the door in the shopping plaza if she was running a little late. It meant that Al must have had another bad night. It was okay; they would wait for her.

But the phone call I received this time was at nine in the morning, and it was from my brother.

"Mommy's having trouble breathing, so we're in the hospital."

Concerned but not overly upset, he told me they were going to give her some breathing treatments and he would get back to me.

She said she felt fine; she was just a little dizzy and wanted to go home."

"Why can't they just give me a shot of something and send me home?" she kept asking my brother.

"Mom," he answered in his deadpan, wry voice that only my brother can pull with her. "This is not *Star Trek;* there's no magic shot to cure what's going on with you."

"Hmmpth!" she said, indignant, and I could picture her sitting in the bed, folded arms across her chest.

The day went by and I didn't hear anything, so that I evening I called his cell phone.

"It's not good," he said, his voice cracking now. "Mommy's had a stroke." She hadn't lost any motor skills, wasn't paralyzed, or numb.

Her mind, however, was gone.

When the doctor asked her name, she couldn't tell him. She couldn't tell him the name of the others in the room either. She talked about fairies and snakes and wouldn't eat the food because it was covered with ants, and she wouldn't accept a drink of water from my sister because she thought it was really vodka. My mother didn't drink and didn't want to start then; that was her reasoning.

We called her, each of us on our own, and each of us hung up with our heads spinning as to the sudden loss of our wonderful mother who drove us nuts, each of us in her own way.

She didn't know our names and just said "okay" when we told her we loved her.

For two days and two nights she sat in the bed, telling bizarre stories and seeing things that weren't there.

What was to happen to her, and how would we take care of her? My brother was the only one who lived near her, and we didn't want the enormity of this situation to fall solely upon him.

My uncertainty of what was to happen to her turned to sadness, realizing I didn't have the chance to say good-bye to her. I had a phone conversation lasting a record forty-five minutes two weeks previously, a feat in itself as miraculous. My mother was never one for chitchat or small talk; it was get on, "How are ya? Everybody okay?" and then get off. She was always busy and always had somewhere to go.

The third day all she wanted to do was sleep, and my sister, who had now traveled from California, the first of us to make it there, was convinced she was heading toward a coma.

The doctors tried to be upbeat, saying sometimes the body is miraculous and heals itself, knowing what it needs to do to get better.

We thought they were nuts.

Prayers were called as we eventually told our children, her grandkids, and the friends and relatives that loved her.

Until Saturday morning, I was planning on leaving to say my good-byes, to kiss the cheek of the woman who brought me into the world, who didn't always do what I wanted her to do, and who always stood by me even when I wanted her to just go away.

Dreading the worst when the phone rang, I answered with trepidation.

"You're not going to believe this," my sister said. "She's back."

"What do you mean she's back?"

"Here" she said, handing the phone off to someone else.

"Hi!" said my mother, as if it was a normal day.

"Mom?" I said. "Mom?" She laughed.

"What's my name?"

I asked her, and she told me, laughing again, but it was really her this time.

I asked her how her trip to Venus was.

"Beautiful," she answered, somewhat in awe. "I remember everything that happened, but I couldn't control was I was saying. But it was a peaceful feeling, and I never felt afraid."

"Wow," I answered, praying silently and thanking God for bringing my mommy back, if not for just a while longer.

"Yup," she said then. "Us Irish are pretty tough, you know. I ain't going anywhere. Why don't you write a book about me?" And then they all laughed, the doctors, the nurses, and my siblings, intermittently I'm sure between tears of relief.

I don't know if it was the prayers or karma or the miraculous healing of the human body.

I'll take it.

GRILLED CHEESE SANDWICHES

I have a friend that e-mailed me today with the following: "If I have to referee one more fight between these three kids, I'm gonna lose my mind!"

Boy did that bring back memories.

I asked her if she had a grilled cheese sandwich moment.

She didn't. So I told her mine.

It had been another long winter, and I had just left the doctor's office with what seemed like the hundredth prescription for Amoxicillin, the medicine for earaches.

My kids were four, five, six, nine, and eleven years old at that time, and they seemed to pass the dreaded illness from one to another. At least they took turns.

It seemed like we traveled in a pack back then, since I couldn't ever get anyone to babysit them on such short notice during winter break.

We were headed to a diner, as it was close to suppertime and I was beat. They had been fighting and picking at each other all day, partly because one was out of sorts, partly because they were getting hungry, and mostly because it was boring and Annoy Your Sibling was the game of the day.

They were pros at that game. At halftime they would play the Let's Make Mom Pull Her Hair Out game. That usually occurred in the evening, and that's how I knew it was time for bed. For me.

We had been ushered in and were sitting at the table waiting for the waitress to come to take our order.

I had every intention of getting them a meatloaf dinner, or chicken, or stew, something substantial. It was my way of relieving my guilt over not being home over a hot stove.

It was a busy evening, as everyone else in town had the same idea. It took a little longer than usual for the waitress to come over, and she had only given us our water, which had been spilled several times. Salt shaker contents were all over the table. Straw papers were made into spitballs. Someone was whining because they were hungry. Someone else was antsy because they had to pee for the twelfth time. Ah, the power of suggestion.

Finally I snapped. I sat straight up and made a motion with my hands, like an umpire at a ball game calling a player: "Youuurr'e out!"

"That's *it!*" I hissed in a voice like Boris Karloff. "You're all getting grilled cheese sandwiches. Do you hear me? Grilled cheese sandwiches!"

The whining stopped. Actually they stopped breathing for a minute. They were stunned beyond words.

And then it happened. One of them started to smile.

Then the other started to giggle. Then another started to cough, and before we knew it, we were howling on the floor.

My kids do a mean imitation of their mother, and whenever things started to get tense as they entered the teenage years, one of them would stop, make the umpire motion, and say, "You're all getting grilled cheese sandwiches!"

It never failed to make us stop what we were doing and laugh our butts off 'til we cried.

So my advice to my friend was this: find a grilled cheese sand-wich moment.

If you have kids, you're going to need it.

Every now and then I think about that day and the reaction they had to my frustration. In the big picture, it was just another day of kids being kids.

I'd give anything if they were all together again, fighting and annoying the hell out of each other.

So I go to the diner and I order one for myself.

Somehow, it makes me feel a little better.

THE GRANDNESS OF
GRANDPARENTING

This week was full of fun and anticipation with the onset of the Apple Blossom Festival and the various events associated with it. I was able to witness some of the fun through the eyes of some of my grandchildren this year, for their parents have decided I am okay to leave them with overnight and that I won't let them get kidnapped for ransom.

It was with new eyes as I stood in awe and watched the nine-year-old and eight-year-old as they boarded the rides at the carnival, much braver than their parents had ever been. There was no fear on their faces as they hopped aboard the tilt-a-whirl and came screaming down the giant slide, sometimes backward. The parade was full, filled with wondrous sights and magnificent sounds, and it seemed to be a little different than years past.

I laughed with real surprise as I watched them both secure prizes at the galleries, he winning a life-size Scooby Doo dog by perfectly throwing two balls into a basket without them bouncing out, and she winning a prized Bratz picture by bursting three wayward balloons precisely with darts. Their parents had never won anything, no matter how many times I supplied them with quarters.

Lying on our backs later that evening, we watched the fireworks ignite the night sky, and I cherished the simplicity of just being together on a cool evening in May. Breakfast the next morning at the airport was the crowning event to end a weekend to match no other, for I realized that I was entering a new phase of my life, one I wasn't sure how to handle. My beloved was also a part of this uncharted territory, a new adventure for him indeed. We looked at each other with awe as the realization of what was happening became clearer and clearer. We were grandparents, and it was grand.

We filled them with pancakes and sausage, kisses and sugar, and sent them home.

It's the best job in the world. The grandest.

HANKY

When I was a kid, I was afflicted with annoying hay fever. I would suffer beginning from the first thaw of spring to the first frost of autumn. My eyes would be itchy and red, and under my eyes would swell to almost double the size. My throat would get hoarse, and I wouldn't be able to talk sometimes, and I was a heartbeat away from developing asthma.

The only over-the-counter medication of the day was Allerest, and my mother bought it in one hundred-tab jars. I can still see the tall jar of blue pills sitting in the medicine cabinet, next to the Alka Seltzer and Head and Shoulders shampoo. Although they dried out my saliva glands (causing other problems such as dental and bowel), it did the trick. It usually lasted about four hours, evidence of its effectiveness wearing off shortly before the fourth hour. An alarm clock was set so that I would wake up at 5:30 a.m. to take the first pill, and I was given a baggie with two more to take to school with me.

Although the clock was set for 5:30 a.m., it really wasn't needed. My father was already up, having awakened at 4:00 a.m. to get ready for work. He would get up and cook the two hard-boiled eggs and toast, the same breakfast he ate every day, 'til the day he died at seventy-three years old. He put on his suit and always made sure he had a white handkerchief in his back pocket—and an extra one for me. White and folded in fours, it was part of his outfit every day.

"Here, kid, take this," he'd say, and I'd grab it as I rushed to the bathroom to blow my nose.

Boxes of tissues were worthless, and toilet paper was a waste of money; I went through them both way too fast. A cloth hanky was what I needed. I had always wished that I had dainty, girly type hankies and certainly not a man's handkerchief.

One of my chores when I was a preteen was to iron those damn handkerchiefs. Bingo Mary would supervise.

"You missed a spot," she'd point out, if I didn't iron straight to the corner of the cloth. That was me—always taking the shortest route.

"What's the difference?" I'd argue. "I'm only going to sneeze into it! Then I'm going to stuff it like this!" I'd pick one up and stuff it into my size A bra. I didn't develop womanly curves until I was much, much older. I stood there with one mutant breast pushing out under my sweatshirt.

She'd just look at my mother, who would be choking on her Pepsi by this point. Bingo Mary would just shake her head and go over to the sink to fill up the teakettle with water.

"Heaven help her, Patsy," she'd announce with a touch of a grin. "She's a loony one, she is."

I never did get those dainty girly type hankies. I carried those thick white cotton handkerchiefs everywhere with me. It never occurred to me to just go out and buy my own. By that time, they had become part of my outfit too, just like they had become my dad's. When he died, I snuck one from his bureau drawer. If I put my nose into it, I can still smell his aftershave. I've never washed it.

Nowadays, I get immunology shots. I make sure I dust and try to be proactive as far as food choices and other things that can set me off.

Every now and then, however, the sky will be clear and blue, and the summer breezes will blow just right, spreading the particles my way.

"Here, babe, take this," he'd say, and my beloved will hand me his hanky. Not a white cotton one like my dad's, though, but a bandana. He has a drawer full of them for he, too, is prone to sneezing and wheezing.

I smile as I honk into the soft cloth and wipe my slowly reddening nose and watery eyes. The tears aren't from the allergies but from the act itself. The gesture reminds me of the gentle smile of my father and the devotion to the routine, as was his nature. Every day he puts on his work clothes for work and sticks a bandana in his back pocket.

Folded in fours and part of his outfit.

Un-ironed.

TRADITION WITH A CAPITAL T

Traveling here and there can wear you down, as exciting as it is to wake up in a different place now and then. It felt like it was taking forever for spring to arrive this year, and even when the calendar finally confirmed it, the winds kicked up over the lake and it felt like November again. The older I get, the more I realize how much I relish the warm weather, even though I love the four seasons.

I've come to realize the remedy for the blues is to surround myself with young life, be it gazing at the new buds on trees, bulbs poking their heads up through the hard, winterized dirt, or the laughter of kids. Luckily it was coming close to the annual sleepover at Nana's, coinciding with the Apple Blossom Festival.

My two oldest grandchildren live in the city and a suburb, so coming out to the "country" is an adventure in itself. Out here there's not a lot of TV played, the pace is slower, and the summer brings long, lazy days swimming in the lake.

It is still spring, so apple blossom season and all that brings is in full bloom, pun intended. The Apple Blossom Festival includes a parade, crowing of an Apple Blossom Queen and Princess, a 5K race, carnival, vendors, and the "fly-in" breakfast held on Sunday at the local airport. It is something we've begun to look forward to since transplanting myself here in Wayne County. For those who have grown up with this festival, it is probably not a big deal. Even their grandpa is not marching in the parade this year; business responsibilities have taken him out of town.

But I am a believer in Traditions with a capital T and try to create as many of them as I can. They are the framer and keeper of memories; hopefully good ideas to pass on to the next generation will come from them.

This year the festival was met with cold and rainy weather,

thunder booming, and lightning kept peppering the skies all after-noon. They were not interested in the Saturday parade or the rides at the carnival, hoping perhaps Sunday would be better. What was important was that we were together.

We went to Barnes and Noble, had a nice dinner at Red Robin, and then went to the movies instead. Borrowing an idea from an old friend of mine, I told them that it was time to get up and dance during the rolling credits at the end of the movie. They looked at me as if I'd lost my mind but eagerly joined in when they saw me head to the front of the theatre. Learning to overcome self-consciousness is a gift I can give them; I learned a very long time ago to not let people have power over how I feel and to not take myself too seriously. Seize the moment, no matter how you bad you might be feeling, because everything passes, the good *and* the bad.

I was happy and felt so much better having them around, lis-tening to them laugh and joke together. They are nine and ten years old, an age that when everything is funny and the sillier the better. Soon they will be teenagers and may not be as enamored with spending time in the country or even with each other. So for today, I was grateful for this respite, to wash myself in the love and affection we feel for each other, secretly hoping someday they will pass the tradition on to their own families. It was silly, and it was wonderful.

I felt like dancing in the movie theatre, so we did, and others began to join us. A new tradition was born.

MICHAEL AND THE FICUS PLANT

I have a ficus plant that stands about four feet tall and sits in the corner of my living room.

It was the kind of plant you can buy from a garden store, a bunch of green leaves stuck into potting soil and secured in a green plastic container about three inches around.

When I bought it over twenty years ago, it didn't look much bigger than a small, potted basil plant. I watered it with love and put it on the kitchen windowsill, bathing it in the sun.

Every time I look at it I am amazed it is still around, thick and lush and growing stronger every day, not succumbing to my ineptitude.

I have never been much of a green thumb, and the only plant I have not killed over the years in this hearty warrior. In fact, it has just been replanted to a pot the size of an outdoor trash barrel. It was time.

In 1985 I remembered showing it to a neighbor, so proud of myself. I had nurtured it to be five inches tall.

"If you give it a bigger pot, it will grow even larger!" she advised. "It just needs more room to grow."

Cautiously and slowly, I transferred the ficus plant to a larger container.

It grew twice its size around the small stems in the course of six months. It seemed like it couldn't grow fast enough and was making up for lost time.

My children grew up right alongside this sturdy plant. They watched me as I tended to it, year after year, as I watered it with love.

It eventually made its way off the kitchen windowsill to a place on the coffee table in the living room, to an eventual pot on the floor.

They and it survived transplants to different pots and different houses, each of them breaking off some of the leaves as they grew but surviving the bumps and bruises that were part of their lives, growing into the sturdy trees they would become.

The youngest of my sons and the last to venture out into the world is moving to Virginia this week. His job has transferred him, and it was too good of an opportunity to turn down. The only one left here is navy boy, and soon he will be relocating to Chicago for graduate studies.

As sad as I am for them all to leave, I recognize it is the inevitability of the times we live in, the price of living a good life, and just the adventure of starting life over in a new town or exploring the unknown outside their own little patch of dirt.

I will miss them all, but I know it is time.

My son simply needs a bigger pot in which to grow. I have watered him and his siblings with love, and they are ready to find their own pots in which to grow even bigger and stronger.

Like my hardy ficus plant, I look forward to witnessing when the next transplant will occur.

FRIDAY THE CAT

My mother e-mailed me the other night and asked, "Why don't you write about Friday?"

For my sixteenth birthday, my boyfriend gave me an adult cat instead of a kitten. He gave him to me on a Friday, hence the name. Not very original, but it seemed cool at the time.

I think that if one of my kids' friends gave them a cat out of the blue, I would have shot them, but my mother just seemed to take it in stride. Just like everything else.

Well, the boyfriend was gone after a short time, probably because my father kept referring to him as the *Long-Haired Weirdo* whenever the poor guy came calling.

But Friday lived on. And on. He must have had another name because he was two years old when I got him. But he seemed to adapt.

He had to be an outside cat because I was allergic to the cat hair and dander, but every now and then I would sit outside on the tree swing and just hold him and pet him. That seemed to be enough for him.

If I took too long between visits, he would jump way up on the window ledge of the kitchen window and call for me. The ledge was narrow, so every now and then you would see this orange mass of fur smash up against the windowpane and then suddenly right itself.

After a while he would fall asleep and fall off. Then smash, and you would see the silly thing again.

Thud, to the ground and smash to the window. He could do this for hours.

"God in heaven, Patsy!" Bingo Mary would scream. "Will you

put that cat out of its misery and take it for a ride?" My mother was known for accidentally running over animals.

This cat definitely had nine lives. He was hit by a car, run over by bicycles, unknowingly locked in the garage for two days, ate bug poison, and God knows what else the silly thing did to itself.

He finally died when I was twenty-four, and they buried him in the backyard next to Pepe, the "Holy Rover." I had since long moved away, had a child, and was working for an attorney when I got the news.

"Friday's dead," my mother said, a little crack in her normally strong voice. "Daddy buried him. Say a little prayer. Even Bingo Mary was teary."

I'll always associate cats with expressions of love. My kids always had cats; I just doubled up on my allergy shots. There's something about the soft ball of fur that is soothing to the psyche and calming to the soul.

When I think back to holding him, it reminds me of a simpler time in my life, when all there was to worry about was getting my homework done. Vietnam had not yet touched me; I was happy going to drama club and practicing for the newest play.

I don't know if sixteen-year-olds today have the same luxuries, the same carefree thoughts.

Nowadays I have three dogs and a cat to keep me company when my husband is on the road or involved in a project. Their unconditional love is reminiscent of my babies and the effortlessness of affection. All they want is for you love them, and they will love you back.

Sometimes it takes someone else to remind you of how blessed you are.

Thanks, Mom.

Here's to you, Friday. Say hey to the gang for me.

THE LITTLE GIRL WHO
DIDN'T GIVE UP

I have a daughter that I did not give birth to. In the pecking order of my family, she would be the eldest. She is the daughter of my second husband, from his first marriage. I had heard all about her when I first married my husband twenty-two years earlier. Born in Scotland, she was a sweet, skinny, little red-haired, freckled-faced cherub, with one eye that turned inward. She was his darling girl until she was six years old. Then she vanished.

I didn't meet her until she was a married woman with a child herself. Survivor of a bitter divorce and more hate in a family than I could ever fathom, she had managed to grow up relatively sane and happy. I had heard all about her through the memories of my husband, reliving holidays and getting through the sadness of missing yet another birthday. He had one picture of her that he carried around with him in his wallet. She was a lover of horses and dolls. How cute she was and precious was her memory to him. How my heart would ache to see him suffer.

He would often dream of her, waking up with a face wet with tears. She was discussed only at brief intervals, telling our other children about her, and one day we would all get to meet her. I knew she was constantly on his mind and in his heart. I prayed that one day they would be reunited and end this torture for him.

I suppose in my heart I had always known one day we would meet, but I wasn't prepared for the power of the emotions that arose within me.

On a lazy, mid afternoon day in winter, the phone rang, and I thought it was one of my sisters. Separated only by miles, and as was our routine, someone would call to have a "visit." We always talked for over an hour while the kids were outside, playing in the snow.

Expecting to hear one of the girls, I was unprepared for what was on the other end of the line. It wasn't my sister. At first the voice was low, hesitant, and soft spoken.

"Is my father there?" she asked in a voice I had never heard but dreamed like it would sound. I thought perhaps it was a wrong number, but something about this little voice with a touch of Scottish lilt spoke to my heart in a way I had only heard during the birth of my children.

"I'm sorry, what did you say, dear?" I asked.

My mind started to race. Could it be?

"I'm so sorry to bother you," she started again. "I just thought … I looked this name up in the phonebook … thought maybe, I've been looking for so long … is my dad there?"

I slid to the floor because the air had left my lungs. There was no sound. Somehow I knew. This was the little redhead.

"Hello?" she asked again. "Are you there?"

I was there. Did I dare ask the question for fear of loosing the connection? I didn't want to scare her.

"Is this Karen?" I asked, barely a whisper. I couldn't breathe.

Silence. "Karen, honey, is that you?" I asked again, more firm than I wanted to sound.

"You *know* me?" Her voice started to tremble. "You *know* me, you know who I *am?*"

"You know me?" she said now, practically screaming.

"Oh God. Oh, honey, I know *all* about you," I answered, also crying and screaming now as well. "I know you. I know you. I know you! Where are you calling from?"

It turns out that she and her mother had moved back to Scotland for a short time but returned to the states shortly thereafter. She had grown up down south. Her mother had been able to work odd jobs to support herself and her redheaded angel, even getting the optic surgery needed to repair the left crossed eye. She had been looking for her father for ten years, never giving up after contacting "family" members who had told her they didn't know where he was. She was always searching, even though she had been told time and time again that he had remarried and was not interested in her. But she never gave up. Something in her drove her to keep going until she found him. Their bond was stronger than the dysfunctional extended family it was her misfortune to have been born into.

She gave me her phone number, and I told her I would call her dad at work to let him know. I would leave the next move up to him, but I knew what he would do.

Years have gone by since that wonderful reunion, but she and I have a special bond that will never be broken. She has been welcomed into my heart and is loved as much as my birth children, who readily accepted her as their sister. A beautiful tall redhead, she is a proud woman of integrity, a loving wife and mother. She is someone I am proud to call my daughter and also my friend. We have spent many happy visits together, getting to know her husband, their family, as well as her mother. She is a kind spirit who just got married too young in life. I could relate. She did a beautiful job in raising a fine young woman.

We know that what happened was divine intervention from God. It was not coincidental she found us when she did. She was about to give birth to her second child and was so anxious for them to know us, to know their other grandfather. I am so thankful I was home to answer the telephone that day and to hear that tiny but hopeful voice on the other end who never gave up against so many intentional road blocks set up to dissuade her.

"I'm so happy I found him," she said that day before we hung up. "Thank God I found him. God is good."

"Yes," I said, "you found him. Welcome to your new family. Welcome home, my darling girl."

Love will find a way.

Yes, God is good.

MY MOTHER'S GREEN SNAKE

I was in Sugarland, Texas, this past weekend. It was a nice change from the northeast with temperatures at a balmy ninety-seven degrees all week. I was visiting my seventy-six-year-old mother who had a stroke earlier this year, and she seems to be fine. The only telltale sign of her illness is the long green tube to which she is permanently tethered and which pumps out oxygen directly into her nose, aiding her lungs damaged by years of Winston cigarettes and ceramic dust. A big brown machine sits on the living room floor, and the tube is long enough to follow her throughout the 1,800-square-foot ranch where she has lived since 1980.

I call it the big green snake.

A smaller portable oxygen tank sets her free to travel outside the home for two hours. She calls it her "buddy" and only opens the oxygen flow valve halfway so that she can "save it." I asked her if she thought she was saving the oxygen for the big box she would end up in. My brother always asks, "Did you just eat a big Popsicle, or is your oxygen on halfway? Your tongue is purple." A lot of people might be offended by our sense of humor, and to say it is macabre is an understatement. But that was how we grew up.

She eats a hard-boiled egg every morning like my father did. She has a special pot that she uses, one whose inside lining has been burned away by excessive heat and should have been in the landfill pile ten years ago. "I fill the pot with water, and when the water is gone I know the egg is done." Smiling at my horror-stricken look, she adds, "Don't worry, I know I can't stand too close with the oxygen on; don't want to blow myself up." How about the entire house? She shrugs and tells me not to be so dramatic.

This house is not the house of my childhood, but memories abound here as we sit in the kitchen and talk about childhood, hers and mine, and how we survived it all as well as each other. The rooms are filled with finished and unfinished ceramic figurines and molds; a large kiln sits in the living room, placed there while she was closing her store of twenty-nine years. In the midst of closing, she took her short foray into Venus, and she was astounded to see all she had collected upon her return to earth. Her friends, my brother and sister-in-law have surrounded her with all that she was familiar to help make the transition back. It didn't take long and was the perfect medicine.

We laugh now at things we thought were traumatic and wondered how we lived through the things that really were. Alcoholism visited us constantly, like a wayward and errant cousin, showing up on the doorstep unannounced and unwelcome. Grandparents, aunts, uncles, and cousins—they were all afflicted, and she did not want to become a card-carrying member of the club. She never touched a drop. She is adamant about not becoming a burden and does not want to live with any of her children.

"I want to die in my own bed," she said out of the blue one morning. She began to tell me things she wanted me to know, a confessional of sorts, and I knew where she was headed.

"Your father talked about things like this when he knew he was dying," she said thoughtfully. "Perhaps I am dying soon." It didn't seem to bother her.

"You're not going anywhere until I step on your snake," I told her, and we laughed while she poured me another cup of hot Tetley tea.

That's the kind of childhood I had. Laughter was the key to survival, and she taught me to be strong the best way she knew how. By example.

This is the memory I want to keep of her, for I know I will probably not see her again. I am not as strong as her and can't bear to not see her sitting at her worktable, head bent forward and eyes focused on a ceramic piece to which she is putting finishing touches. A strong light creates a halo around her now white-haired head, thin and wispy as she looks up at me for a moment and smiles. She knows too that we are saying good-bye, and it is all right. She is happy and finally at peace. Somehow, all the craziness was worth it.

SILLY STORIES

DUCK LOVE

This is how pathetically organized I am.

I have divided my friends into categories, and I have even given the categories names. This information comes as no surprise to them, and it doesn't seem to bother anyone. They accept this quirk I have and love me anyway. Okay, maybe it is a bit anal.

One of the groups is called simply "The Ducks." However, we arrived at this title together. The six of us met while working at a bank downtown many years ago. Even though most of us have moved on to other jobs and even other parts of the country, we always kept in touch and had a "Duck Lunch" or a "Duck Dinner" every couple of months. We always made it a point to meet at Christmas time and have a "Christmas Duck Dinner." Not every one of us could meet for the lunch or the dinner, but nobody ever missed the Christmas Duck Dinner. None of us orders duck, by the way. It would be too cannibalistic.

How did we come up with this moniker? One lunchtime meeting we were discussing our kids and the cute but embarrassing things they do sometimes. One woman was explaining how she met her new neighbors. "Remember the cartoon *Darkwing Duck?*" she began. "Remember how the character was a superhero and just before he would pounce on a villain, he would yell, 'Suck gas and die, evildoer'?" We all nodded because it was such a stupid cartoon and since most of us had boys it was something we had to view regularly. "Well," she went on, trying to contain herself while a grin tugged at her mouth, "my new neighbors were moving into the house next door to me, and we were chatting on their lawn as the movers brought in their furniture. All of a sudden, here comes my six-year-old son with a blanket wrapped around his neck like a cape, pretending he's flying." She rolls her eyes at the memory. "I called to him to come over to us so I could introduce him to our new friends. As he lands at the foot of my neighbor and I am about to announce my pride and joy, he screams out, "Suck *ass,* evildoer!" They looked at him, then at me, then back at him, and went into the house. We only wave hello at Christmas."

Needless to say, we were howling on the floor by the time she got the final words out, tears rolling down our faces. We were laughing so hard, people started coming over to us to find out what was so funny. So she would have to tell the story again, and by this time none of us could breathe.

So we simply became the Ducks.

Christmas is a great time for the Ducks. It's a time to catch up with one another. The highlight of this dinner is when we give each other gifts. These are not just any gifts, they have to have a duck theme, and they have to be under ten dollars. You would be amazed the things out there with a duck connection. But it's more than just having a laugh with a couple of girlfriends. Sometimes it's a real effort to get together because it just doesn't fit in to our busy sched-ules. We sometimes have to schedule and reschedule these lunches, and it is because of the diligence of one particular Duck that we do finally meet. She won't let us forget how important we are to one another. We have been through many things together over the years. Even though all six of us may have not been together at the same time, whoever's there fills in the blanks that our boyfriends, husbands, and kids can't fill.

We don't compete with one another. We give each other advice when asked, and even if it isn't. We don't talk about each other when one of us isn't there. We laugh about bad haircuts and incom-petent bosses. We listen to the different stages of romance and the lamentation of wondering where all the good men are. We don't complain about who paid more on the check. We talk about mov-ies and books and how we would have changed the ending. We celebrate the marriage of a son or daughter or the arrival of a baby, whichever comes first. It doesn't matter to us; we don't judge.

We are there for each other when our hearts get broken, be it by men, parents, or children. When we lose jobs, there's no lecture or I-told-you-so looks. I know this fact the best because I think I hold the record of losing the most jobs. Hell, I lost a whole company once, but that's another story. We take care of each other.

The point is this. It's simple. We take so many things for granted. Our quality of life is just so because someone made the effort to ensure it would be so. It is the same with friendships. Make the effort to keep quality friendships. It's worth it. Even if you have to name the friendship, it's worth it. Even if you think you're being pathetic, so what? Who cares? You're with the Ducks. *Quack, quack.*

TURTLE DAVE

Dave was a turtle who was also a hopeless romantic.

He stood somewhat bigger than lake turtles, and his shell was black and shiny, not like the ordinary green of his friends. He was much rounder than some of his fellow turtle citizens, a fact that was made much more obvious when he stuck his long, scrawny neck out of the shell.

Quiet but not necessarily shy, he was a thinking man's turtle. He didn't say much, but when he did, it invariably surprised the listener. It was going to be profound. Adding to the studious effect, he was nearsighted, thus requiring the use of eyeglasses. He wore wire-rimmed round spectacles that increased the size of his eyeballs, should he look into the face of another.

A middle-aged fellow in turtle years, he had never married and had no turtle kids.

He was hopelessly in love. He adored the most beautiful pelican in the world, his heart very nearly bursting out of his shell every time he saw her! Her long dark hair hung down to the small of her back, her wings smooth and silky. Her long legs would glide effortlessly against the wind as she flew. Whenever she flew by him close to the shore, Dave thought he might faint, so quick would his heart begin to pound against his shell, rendering him breathless and dizzy.

Romaine. Her name was Romaine.

Romaine was tall and regal, her feathering that of a pale blue, shining like sea glass against the light of the bright morning sun. She was different from the other pelicans, who were mostly white and gray. She liked to take her breakfast along the shore, flying low to the ground to see if she could spy any small minnows. She was very health conscious and had learned to watch her weight. Minnows would be fine.

Scouring the water, she didn't see Dave until she came to rest upon a rock. Standing on a rock, one leg pulled up against her abdomen while standing comfortably on the other as pelicans do, she began her morning meal. She didn't notice it took Dave close to forty-five minutes to travel close enough to enable her to hear him. He was, after all, a turtle.

Wiping her beak with her strong left wing, she was about to lift off from the rock she had been dining upon when she noticed him.

She was immediately self-conscious and wondered if she looked fat.

This is one good-looking turtle, she thought to herself, *and smart too.* She had heard all about him from her pelican girlfriends, who had noticed him over the years. He always seemed to be surrounded by other good-looking turtle girls, and she sighed slightly as he crawled closer to her.

He would never be interested in me, she thought and resigned herself to being alone for yet another cold winter.

Dave finally made his way as close to the lovely Romaine as his poor constitution would allow. His heart was beating madly, and his palms were sweaty. He could barely look at her, his eyeglasses fogged by his heavy breathing.

Oh no! he thought in a panic. She had daintily stepped off the rock, and she was coming toward him ever so slowly. He had to grab hold of a nearby seashell to prevent himself from falling over.

Whatever should I say to him? the nervous pelican thought. She missed the solidarity of her pelican friends standing behind her. Usually when she was in a crowd she was much braver when it came to looking for a mate. She was on her own now, no birds frolicking in the sea shore beside her, laughing at every witty joke or small talk that came out of her mouth.

What shall I do? she thought frantically, and they inched closer and closer toward each other. She racked her brain desperately for some intelligent conversation opener, something that would make him laugh, thus putting her at ease. *But what the heck do turtles think is funny?*

They were but inches apart when Dave stopped to look up at

the sky into the eyes of his beautiful princess, his darling Romaine. Golden streaks of sunlight shone through her blue feathers, creating an almost angelic outline of her svelte frame.

He could not speak.

Neither did she.

They looked at each other, a thousand words not spoken, a million thoughts left hanging in the sunlight.

Turtle Dave nodded and cleared his throat and said … nothing.

Romaine the beautiful pelican belied no emotion but fluttered her eyelashes. Disappointment loomed big in her heart, but she was too proud to say anything in reply.

She watched the turtle as he slowly moved his way up the sand, leaving his indentation of his trail behind him. It was the only remembrance of the fact that he had been there at all.

Small tears formed in the corner of Romaine's eyes as the form of the turtle blended in with the horizon. She watched until it was gone.

I knew it! She shuddered. *I'm too fat. Why would he ever be interested in me?*

I knew it! he whispered sadly to himself. *I'm too serious. Why would she ever be interested in me?*

And they never felt the depth of their feelings for each other, never experienced the joy of a union, or felt their warm breath upon their necks.

Because they never uttered a word to each other again.

Unrequited love stinks. If you're interested in someone, say hello.

It all starts with hello.

You might be wrong about what you *think* you know.

But you *won't* know unless you say it.

Good luck.

THE THINGS YOU SEE WHEN YOU DON'T HAVE A CAMERA

I swear to you the next few sentences are true.

I have been known to embellish a situation from time to time, although I never outright lie. But it was amazing to me the things I've seen since yesterday and was not able to document.

Actually it started Thursday of last week. My beloved came walking into the house, shaking his head and laughing.

"You won't believe what I just saw," he said after pecking a quick one on my cheek.

"What's that, dear?" I answered absentmindedly, as I was interested in starting the paragraph for a column.

"A rooster!"

We live in the country, so I wasn't understanding the awe in his voice. I looked up at him. He was waiting for a reaction.

"A rooster?"

"Yeah, a rooster. On a stick."

"A stick?" Now he had my attention.

"Yeah. Being held by a guy with a long, scraggly beard."

"A stick being held by a guy with a long, scraggly beard?"

"Yeah!" He was beside himself now with excitement and couldn't seem to believe the words himself as he spat them out.

"A stick being held by a guy with a long, scraggly beard; he was sitting right on it, and the guy was riding a bicycle." He was nearly jumping up and down with incredulous seriousness.

I didn't believe him.

Come Saturday afternoon, we had many errands to run, one of them being the sad event of a funeral service. We've had to go to several the last few days, and the sensation of here we go again was sadly familiar. The weekend before we had buried a much-loved firefighter; he was only fifty-two years old and way too close to our own sense of immortality.

I had put away my camera, as I had covered two assignments for the paper, and left it on my desk, a faithful companion that I thought I would give a rest after using it all week.

It was as we were turning the bend of the road to town that I saw the figure that had driven my beloved nearly mad with excitement: a tall, scraggly-bearded man riding a bicycle. On his shoulder was a long stick, slung over like a child who was running away from home. I half expected to see hanging from it a ball of clothes, rolled up and tied like a make-believe hobo of the road.

Instead, there sat a rooster, not tied or constrained, sitting on the end of it.

And me without a camera.

I will never put that darn thing away again.

SUMMER DUCKS

Well, the Ducks got together tonight for their annual Summer Duck Fest—the counterpart to the Christmas Duck Gathering. We're a group of seven women who all worked together at a bank many years ago and have kept in touch. It is the testament of what true friendship is all about.

One by one we lost our jobs at the bank, until only one is left working there.

But through the years, the Ducks have remained friends and fierce allies when it came to battling the outside world. We have been there for each other through divorces, remarriages, deaths, births, grandchildren, and child-rearing horror stories. The teen-age years were particularly painful for some of us, and we leaned on those who had survived it first. We were our own best friends, filling the need when a gap opened, our laughter a warm, balmy swathe for our souls.

If you're thinking this is going to be a column about a group of middle-aged women whooping it up, read on.

This was the year several of us turned fifty years old, a monumental event worthy of some kind of celebration. Mindful that some of our Duck sisters were not as adventurous as others, the three birthday girls put their heads together to see what could be done to commemorate such an occasion.

"We could go mountain climbing!" said Adventure Duck. "I'm teaching a survival course now, did you know that?"

The other birthday Duck and I just looked at her and then at each other, pretending we didn't hear her.

"Geneva Duck wouldn't stand for that, and you know that Lady Duck wouldn't be caught dead in a tent!" I said matter-of-factly.

The Other Writer Duck shook her head in agreement.

"And you know Las Vegas Duck just wants to stay around and

play with her triplet grandchildren," she said, winking at us both. Las Vegas Duck spends six months here in the east and then travels to the west to be with her "other" friends.

Just then Accountant Duck called on Adventure Duck's cell phone.

"Where are we going for dinner this year?" she asked. "I need to write it down so I don't forget."

"Tell her to tattoo it on her hand!" Other Writer Duck said, and we all laughed.

A lightbulb went off above Adventure Duck's head.

"Hey," she said with a sly smile forming across her lips. "Are you thinking what I'm thinking?"

So six weeks ago, on a Wednesday night, three fifty-year-old Ducks went on an adventure, to a place they never thought they would go: a tattoo parlor, to have a three-inch yellow rubber duckie tattooed on their left shoulders.

God only knows what we'll do when we're seventy-five.

ANIMAL STORIES

MY FIRST TIME

It was my first time.

Lunch packed and sent off with a kiss, my beloved had left for work, allowing me to complete the morning rituals of cleaning up and feeding the dogs and our embattled old cat, Zeekee.

But I knew today would be like no other day, for I was also left to accomplish the task I knew he could not bear to do. It was the Tuesday before Thanksgiving, a time of thanks and gratitude.

Our appointment wasn't until 2:00 p.m., so I had time to prepare us all.

The dogs' feather bed had become a place of solace for her threadbare, nearly skeletal body. She had lost a considerable amount of body fat, and her skin just hung from her frame. She was always cold now, and I had taken to wrapping her in a blanket to keep her warm on cold mornings. They took turns lying with her and licking her head.

Most often she would wait patiently in line to be fed, knowing I took care of her brothers first, watching and waiting, sometimes grabbing a sip from the community water bowl they all shared. The boys gave her a wide berth now as they watched her slowly pander over to the dish, now looking mammoth-like against her impoverished frame. She drank slowly, as if to savor the taste, since this had become the only thing she was able to keep down.

I had wondered how I would transport her to the destination, as she hated riding in the car and didn't like to be handled. I thought of putting some bath hand towels in a small plastic tub. I placed it on the couch, where it laid there waiting for her for several hours.

Throughout the morning, she systemically walked from room to room, slowly and deliberately, before she made her decision to wash herself in the makeshift bedding.

She was looking for him to say good-bye, and my eyes began to well up at the realization she knew what was to follow.

She jumped right in among the towels, thankful again for the warmth. It was as if she knew the makeshift bed would be a welcome method of travel, since her legs were now wobbly and shaky.

After starting up the car and letting the heat blast throughout the vehicle, I placed her on the passenger seat. Putting the car in gear, I backed up slowly out of the drive so as not to startle her in the sudden shift in direction. Her little head poked between the towels, and she watched me with her tired eyes the entire trip. More than once I had to cover her head gently as if to beckon her to rest, for I couldn't bear to watch her watch me.

Barely two minutes before our arrival, she got a burst of energy and jumped out of the box! It was so surprising I had to pull over to retrieve her from the backseat.

"What is this?" I admonished her gently with a sad smile, and "You'll catch your death ..." caught in my throat as I covered her back up.

The greeters solemnly ushered us in, and my swollen eyes needed no explanation. They knew why we were there and had done this many times before.

"This is my first time ..." I offered lamely, and the one in charge put her arm around me and kissed my cheek.

"You can stay with her as long as you need," she offered, and we went to the room with a countertop covered in quilts and bathed in dim lights.

Kneeling down to look face-to-face, I stroked her back gently as they administered the first injection, the one that would begin to take the pain away. Like a soldier on a battlefield, she crawled slowly on her belly in an attempt to get closer to me so that we could wait together cheek-to-cheek. My tears fell on her soft fur, and I answered the ringing cell phone that was in my pocket. It was him, and he was crying softly, waiting for the inevitable.

The fur on her bony leg was shaved gently and the final injection complete; I kissed her pink nose while stroking her head. As I looked into her eyes one last time, I watched her slowly fade away, until the light in her eyes went out. Knowing she had no more pain and was never to be hungry again, I said good-bye to our brave warrior feline.

"It's done," I whispered to him and promised to bring her home to him soon.

KISS ME GOOD-BYE

It's funny to see the similarities between my "children" now and my children from another time.

One by one they ask to go out. While standing by the front door, it's the signal to all that they need to do some business. "Let me out, Ma. I got work to do."

I kiss them good-bye upon the tops of their furry heads, not unlike I did with my other children.

One by one as they went off to school in the morning, they stood at the door. En masse they ran out, but not until I ruffled their hair or buzzed them on the cheek. Back then first came breakfast, be it either cereal or scrambled eggs—I always made sure they had something in their bellies.

Nowadays it's cereal or breakfast bones in less discriminating bellies.

Eager to get to the task at hand, they went bounding out the door.

Not because they were anxious to get to school. It was the place where their friends were, their comrades in arms to battle another day. Of all the things I know I did wrong in this life, I am proudest of what I did right. My children have lifelong friends, born out of growing up in the same neighborhood, something almost unheard of in this day and age.

With the uncertainty of the financial climate, job security, and just plain wanderlust, families are spread apart more than ever. My own siblings, as well as my mother, all live in different states, and it is at the holiday times that I miss them the most. I know it is the natural progression of life that my children will spread their wings and move on to somewhere else; in fact, it's already started. Three boys and three girls, they've all left me in their own way. Just as I know that one day my children here will also go off to somewhere else, I am content to have this time with them, as little as it may be. Life moves at backbreaking speed if you let it; always take time to kiss the ones you love good-bye. Give them a pat on the head and a dog bone while you're at it. I let them out, one by one, to go see their friends in the neighborhood. They all know they are blessed to be where they are. I know that I am.

RAISING CAIN-INE

Although it can be said there are similarities between raising children and raising animals, there are some distinct differences between them. That being said, however, it is realistic to note just how human our four-legged friends have become.

Dogs have been man's best friend for centuries. I never thought they would become mainstream, part of the landscape, especially in my life.

There are dogs that have jobs, like the search-and-rescue variety. They can sniff out baggage carriers of substances they have been trained to find. They alert us to danger and comfort us when we're down. More and more often I am seeing dogs that go with their masters to their jobs. A law firm I worked in had an old mutt that came to work every day. She was a black Labrador mix with gray around her face, and her gait was slow and calculated. I could imagine her thinking, *Okay, this foot there, this foot here, that's it. Ahhh, there's my corner,* as she'd go lie down in a sunny spot of the reception area.

They can have their trials, just like any teenager. They may not like the dog food you're giving them laced with flea medicine. They may not like the new collar you got them, and their displeasure reminds me of when I was still able to pick the kids clothes out.

"I'm not wearing that old lady dress!" the youngest daughter would yell to me when I would make her dress for church.

"I'm not tucking my shirt tail in!" the middle son would say when dressing for dinner out, to eat at a restaurant other than a McDonald's, and I see it again every time I admonish my younger pups to stay inside the fence.

But like all siblings, they took care of each other, looked out for one another.

Imagine my surprise when one of the older boys said he saw his younger sister in the car with a group of kids but that he had "taken care of it."

"I told her to get her butt home!" he announced proudly as she came walking in sheepishly behind him. They both walked to the TV room, plopped on either end of the couch, and promptly fell asleep, but not before giving each other a playful punch in the arm.

Last week, I was greeted by our oldest dog, Riley, barking loudly and consistently, as I was getting out of the shower. It felt more like stepping out of a *Lassie* episode.

"What is it, boy?" I chided him, half serious.

When he wouldn't stop, I realized he was serious.

I looked around and couldn't find his little brothers, JJ and Simon. Big brother went to the screen door and pushed his nose against the screen to open it. Walking outside, he barked again, and I was able to see what he was calling me for.

There stood his little brothers, soaking wet.

They had gotten out of the gate and went swimming in the lake, all by themselves.

Riley walked in with his head in the air, looking at me as if to say, "Kids! I told them to get their butts home!"

JJ and Simon came walking in sheepishly behind him.

They all went to their places in the family room and lay down, but not before giving each other a big shake, lake water flying everywhere. Within minutes they were asleep.

Some things never change.

GRACE

There are angels all around us everywhere, and never do we see them more vividly than at Christmas time.

Angels are known for acts of kindness and mercy, for opening their loving arms and enveloping those in their wings who need them in times of trial or sorrow. Angels carry the messages of peace and hope, a soothing balm for pain or suffering. They remind us that we are human, we are flawed, and that most importantly, we are all connected.

There is a particular angel in our neighborhood who is so very humble she didn't want me to write this story, so modest she doesn't want those around here to know her name. She and her family feel they have done nothing special; they were just in the right place at the right time. It is with grace they acknowledge this act of kindness, and so that is what I will call her.

Grace.

They didn't know how long he had been lying in the road. He was the victim of a hit-and-run car accident, and they thought him dead; they were going to give him a proper burial.

"He was just lying there," Grace recounted to me. "But when I touched him to pick him up, he opened his eyes!"

Several visits to the veterinarian proved to be very encouraging, as Grace and her family nursed the animal back to life. It was not known if he was a cat who had used all his lives, but it is safe to say it was as if he was brought back from the dead.

They named him Lazarus.

Nowadays you can see him traveling with Grace as she does her chores for the day. He stays particularly close by, as you would imagine, for she has been his protector and redeemer. Lazarus stays very close.

He sits on her right shoulder like a parrot.

With neither fear nor hesitation he sits atop Grace, towering over others as she walks down the road. With complete trust in the one who has raised him from the dead, he sits tall and calm as they walk down the lane on a journey together of their own choosing.

Whether they are off to the post office, the local fire hall, or whatever destination she chooses, they are greeted with a smile and welcomed with arms opened wide.

What a sight to behold, the angel and her cat, the luckiest animal in the world.

Yes, there are angels all around us everywhere, but never more evident than at Christmas. Angels who perform those acts of kindness lovingly, quietly, and without fanfare, wanting nothing in return.

May we always be open to acknowledge the Graces in our lives; even better, become Grace-like ourselves.

It is the greatest gift one can give to another.

Love.

BONE CRUMBS

There's a certain time in the evening after dinner, when the dogs are fed, or the company's gone home, and the dishes are done. The world has calmed down and the birds are getting ready for bed, along with the chipmunks, turtles, and seagulls. It is a time when everyone slows down, and the twilight descends through the living room with the setting of the sun, another day gone by. The dogs lie at our feet and chew on a rawhide bone, and they glance over at one another from time to time to see if there is a remnant of any bone crumbs the other has left. I have no name for it yet, but it stands apart from the rest of the day.

Not every day has this quiet time, for some days are better than others; this was not a good one.

I suppose it's good that God gives us bad days as well as good ones; it's probably so we can appreciate the better days when the bad ones finally leave.

We sit, drinking some wine, looking out the picture window as the snowflakes begin to gather one by one. They pile themselves upon the grill on the deck, a sad reminder of when the wind was warm and the breezes cool, not cold like the frigid arctic blasts this evening.

There is a certain reassurance, however, as we sit silently, with no music or TV blaring in the background. The only sound is the breathing of sleeping dogs, the big one at our feet, the smaller one lying across both our laps.

As I snuggle close to my beloved, my rock and my confidant, I am reminded of what first drew me to him in the first place. Crop circles and landmines are covered by the mounds of snow for now, but they are waiting for us both when the first signs of spring.

There's no need for tears, for his arms around me are strong and reassuring; all I need do is breathe.

The good days are on their way back, as sure as the sun will rise in the morning. The blues will have played themselves out, and the sunrises will once again warm our faces as we sit, together, watching the dogs run to the lake. Of that I have no questions; no doubts to sidetrack us.

And in the evening, they will sit beside us, looking for crumbs from the other.

Once again, the crop circles and landmines will make themselves known.

And I will smile at my beloved in the sun, happy in the knowledge that we are together forever.

IT REALLY IS OKAY

Turning eight years old in my family was to be celebrated.

Way past what psychologists refer to as the "age of reasoning," they were now allowed to do things a little differently than when they were age seven. This was especially meaningful for the last three of my children, who were born one year after the other.

Eight years old meant they were allowed to stay up a little later than their siblings, hang out with their older brother, who was twelve, and watch *Knightrider* on Tuesday nights.

But crossing this threshold also meant they were assigned different chores. Already responsible for making their bed by age four, the graduation to "kid" from "little kid" was monumental. Now they had to bring their laundry to the laundry room, help set the table, and clear it after dinner. They did it without arguing or pressure, and they seemed to like being part of the routine of running a household full of people.

The most impressive upgrade in their young lives was the ability to go to summer camp—two weeks in August at the YMCA summer program. After passing the swimming tests (at the Y where they had taken lessons the year before), they timidly stuck one toe into a world without Mom and ventured off on their own for a while.

They watched each other year after year leave the cocoon of the minivan, complete with a duffel bag full of clean shorts and bathing suits, knapsacks with army men, and pieces of home. Memories of the older children ahead of them who had stories galore to share were at the forefront. Excitement mixed with terror, they could not wait until it was their turn.

Over a small, sunburned shoulder, they looked at me one more time for confirmation. *"Is this really okay?"* And I smiled with a tinge of sadness. "*Yes, it really is.*" And they dashed off to find their bunk in a cabin assigned to them.

As the summers passed and they grew older and stronger, there were no longer tearful looks exchanged as they left the nest for new adventures. It was now so very uncool to miss Mom and Dad, and I barely got a note more than two lines long. I knew this was how it was supposed to be, but I was saddened anyway.

Years have flown by, and they have all left the nest and created memories of their own and each other, reminiscing fondly about summer camp and their adventures they shared. I hug myself inside as I sit and watch them as they talk about sending their children to summer camp when they are ready.

Leaving town for various work functions, my beloved and I have finally found the right kind of summer camp for our boys, three Labs ages three, four, and six.

A lovely kennel run by the woman we call Grandma. When it is time to go, they jump excitedly into the back of the car, complete with their own knapsacks filled with treats and toys and memories of home.

They are tearful as they look over their shoulders to make sure it is really okay to leave us, and we smile with a touch of sadness as we confirm to them and say, "Yes, it really is okay."

Everything is as it should be.

MAPLE LEAF SOUP

I've written many stories regarding the escapades of a dog named Riley. He's usually the smart and sensible side of a conversation with my alter ego and alias, Emeline. I've shared with you the musings of the teenage felines Eleanor and Simmons and the aristocratic air of Zeekee, a beautiful and worldly cat.

There have been many stories of imaginary animal characters, magical, talking creatures of the air, the land and of the sea, all living in the Kingdom of Doolittle. I used them all as metaphors to display the immeasurable kindness of humanity and the insatiable desire of the soul to do good, sometimes amongst the stranger and sometimes in heartfelt acts of love for their neighbor.

Mostly they were conversations in my head. A way to convey a message of hope and faith to those closest to me, a nod in their direction or a slight scolding as to what they were currently doing in their life at the moment.

They were things that I would never say to them, but Emeline could.

All these creatures were imaginary, but some among them have become real, serving as a gentle nudging of love and commitment to beings that could not live alone and ask for little to survive, giving much love in return.

But before there was Riley, before Eleanor and her sassy sister, Simmons, and before the queen and Emeline's nemesis, Zeekee, there was someone else.

Before them all, there was Jack.

Jack was the black Labrador retriever that changed my life, even though he had passed away long before I met him.

Black Jack Riley was his full name. He was the subject of another's writing, a loving tribute to a faithful companion who brought much joy to those around him, especially those closest to him. He was put down on a cold winter's day in an act of compassion but breaking the hearts of those who loved him. The tale of the loss brought tears to my eyes, a shocking surprise to myself and to others who knew me.

I've pictured him in my mind as the kindly old grandfather that everyone loved, walking slowly down the gravel lane to the lake and laying down amongst the cool rocks on the shore. I can see him in my mind's eye as he and his master strolled during their daily constitution. I can imagine the love his master washed over him as he got more crippled and infirm as the weeks wore on, finally barely able to walk at all.

But I can also picture this animal of grace as a younger, sturdier, livelier Adonis of the canine world.

Jumping high with all fours outstretched and catching biscuits thrown in midair with his mighty jaws, what a spectacle of health and athletic exuberance he must have been! His shiny black coat glistening in the sun, strong legs to propel him zig-zagging back and forth as he played fetch or tug-of-war with a rope.

But there must have been a playful and mischievous side to him as well. Sitting in the passenger seat of the local fire company's fire truck in many a Fourth of July parade, he would reign as the king of all station dogs, proudly displaying fake antlers at Christmas or a yellow fire chief hat, loving the attention and adoration.

Jack was the kind of dog that was adored by animal lovers and even those less trusting of his ilk. Never threatening, his master would have to search house by house to call his errant son home. *Come back and visit us again tomorrow, Jack!* they would call after him as he would traipse down their driveway and into the arms of his laughing "dad."

As they traveled in the autumn to their favorite haunts, there were many memories made as years went by. A dog of inquisitive nature, Jack would always stop at a puddle full of maple leaves and get a drink.

"I noticed he would always look up and wait for me to say what I always said." His "dad" would laugh as he recalled the memory to me. "And he wouldn't move until I muttered the words. I swear he knew what I was saying."

"And what was that?" I would ask; even though I knew the answer, I never tired of the telling.

The man would smile sadly and say it once more, as if it was yesterday.

"Oh boy, a big pot of maple leaf soup, eh, Jack? And then I'd throw him another biscuit."

The man would talk to him all the time, and Jack would talk back.

It was the description of the dog that drew me to the man, to this place, to this new life that I have, living in the Kingdom of Doolittle. Never known to be a dog lover myself, the story of Jack made such an impression on me that I knew I had to know the person who had experienced such profound love and wanted to share it with others. I began to feel that love myself when he taught me how to talk to the animals too.

If all dogs go to heaven, I know that I will want to meet up with him and share a pot of maple leaf soup. I'm sure he will let me run with him, and I will ask him all kinds of questions about his life down on earth and the secret to his tenderness, the ability to change the lives of those around him.

For he certainly changed mine. Surely an angel in heaven now, I'll quote my friend, the man, and say you are the "Catcher of Slow Rabbits."

The Lord sends us friends and companions when we need them most, helpers to aid our battered and withered souls when we are lonely, to make us smile when we are down and to show us love when we feel unlovable.

Gifts from above. Black Jack Riley sent me mine.

.

SPIRITUAL STORIES

CHURCH OF THE ST. BAIT
AND HOLY TACKLE

It was a longtime hangout for fishermen, beach dwellers, and sun worshipers.

The building itself, no bigger than a fishing shack when it first opened, was an institution.

It stayed open year round, even in the dead of winter.

It was there to accommodate the brave ice fisherman who happily cut circles in the ice-covered lake and sat in an equally small box on the cold block, gloved hands around a piping hot cup of coffee.

It was there during heat waves to soothe the many faces clamoring for relief, whether with an ice pop to slurp, a cold beer to quench, or an ice cream sandwich to satisfy.

The busiest day was always Sunday, and I thought it a little sad. Up at the crack of dawn, I wondered aloud, "Why didn't these people go to worship; why would they rather be fishing?"

The morning finds the hangout filled to capacity, especially in the makeshift cafeteria. The years had been kind to the business, but the only indication the place was making any money was the constant additions to enlarge the structure. Rooms appeared, one after the other, not in any particular order or traffic pattern. It was as if a hole in the wall was paved through to make way for another set of tables.

The breakfast menu consisted of coffee, juice, bagels, and donuts. The last few years found the owner cooking up a side of eggs over easy and hash browns, but that was the extent of the entrees offered. It was primarily a bait and tackle store, a place to meet up with your buddies, grab a pack of smokes and a pail of bait, and attend to the business at hand—fishing.

I started passing by the shack when I walked the boys for their morning exercise. Not fully awake myself, I would venture inside to be greeted by the strong aroma of coffee beans and old boots. In the summer the fans were blowing full speed, the winter warmed by a wood stove; there was no air-conditioning for cooling or heating ducts to warm your feet over. No one seemed to mind.

As I sat down at a card table, the waitress/owner poured my cup of steaming hot coffee silently but with a smile. There wasn't really anything that needed to be said that early in the morning. The sun had yet to rise.

One by one, the fishermen came inside, helping themselves to a cup of coffee on the stove and grabbing a pail of bait. Clouds of smoke followed them wherever they walked, the smell of tobacco and aftershave permeating the small room. Some wore high wading boots; others dressed in yellow slickers. It was Labor Day weekend, and the weather had turned cool, reminding us of autumn's arrival. Fishing was at its premium now, for the waters would soon become choppy and the waves challenging.

One of the men lifted his cup up to the woman as she poured the last of the coffee from the urn.

"Blessings," he said simply.

"Have a good one," she answered, and they both bowed their heads, as if in prayer.

My face belied the questions I held in my heart; *Praying for fish?* I thought.

"It's a great way to greet the Lord in the morning," she said kindly.

"Watching the sunrise in your boat, quiet and calm surrounding you, you can't help but feel the hand of God all around." Others behind the man stood beside one another nodding their heads.

"Amen" was said in unison. "Amen."

The old shack burned down last summer. It was the victim of one too many tar additions to the roof, and the owners were lucky the thing went up during the night and not earlier in the morning. It was thought ancient electric wiring was mainly the culprit. No one knew for sure.

Meanwhile, the insurance companies involved took their time in assessing the damage, not sure whether to total the structure or let her refurbish. Tearing it down might erase the fact that it was ever there in the first place, for the old woman who raised it like her child was getting tired. She operated out of a makeshift tent this summer, but it is unknown what the future will bring. For all we know it might be replaced by a shiny new diner or a Starbucks coffee shop.

I am thankful that I was able to get to the place before it was completely gone, for it was as holy and reverent as any church building in these parts. I was reminded once again that it doesn't matter where you pray; what matters is that you do.

The Church of the St. Bait and Holy Tackle.

Worshiping at its purest.

HOW MUCH

I wonder how God picks the burdens we have to carry.

How do we end up with the unwanted trials that are thrust upon our shoulders, and when does he decide we are rid of them? Is he up there with a clipboard and crossing off each pound as it is assigned, erased when it is completed or when he thinks we've had enough?

Why are various trials so heavy for some, almost unbearable, while others' seem to be a minor inconvenience? How does he determine who gets what?

I think the more you struggle, the bigger the burden. Why? Because if you have carried something so horrendous on your shoulders and it hasn't destroyed you, it means you have learned something from it. It means that you are stronger than when you started. You are ready to show others what it takes to come through the other side of a nightmare.

Why would God put children through horrible abuse? Why would he cause such suffering for the parents, the siblings? We'll never know until we see him. But I also believe we are vessels, tools God uses to teach us to learn from one another. To be an aide to one who is also suffering and cannot shoulder the pain alone is probably the deepest gift of love one can offer to another.

I am not saying we need to take the burden completely off the shoulders of the person in pain. There is a reason for it, and we shouldn't presume we know why. We are there to aid without question, to assist without resentment, and to help without prodding. Relief comes from above, not from us. True love in its purest form. We are here to love all who walk the earth, not just those whom we recognize.

How does one carry their burdens? Are we vocal martyrs, complaining of our loads and envying others' seemingly lighter ones? Do we bemoan how difficult our trials are and why they are so unfair? Do we look downward, a visible sign for all to see that we are overwhelmed and tired?

Or do we just carry them, shifting them from one shoulder to the other when the need arises? Holding our heads up, face smiling toward the sun and to heaven, appreciating the beauty of the day. Accepting the task at hand. To be thankful we can carry anything at all.

When one burden is lifted, do we make room for another or hope that we are finished and have paid our share?

Or does God say, "Good. You handled that well. Now, have some more."

Is it all right to say, "Take this from me; it's too much; I can't handle any more. I need help."

I think it is.

But you'll never know for sure until you ask.

PURPLE OF ANOTHER COLOR

For all intents and purposes, it seems I began my life and settled it all within the contents of a suitcase.

I've written about it before, both metaphorically and literally. I called it *The Purple Suitcase,* and it was mainly a compilation of my thoughts, with the *Pollyanna* happy ending that my true love would know enough to tell me to put it away, my need to question and search was over. I had not yet met Stephen.

Purchased in 1972, to begin what I thought was going to be the first of many traveling adventures, it was the first thing I packed when I eloped.

Several years later, it is what I used to take what was of value with me to travel across the country, another grand adventure to my twenty-two-year-old mind.

The following year I moved to Philadelphia for a job, young son and purple suitcase in tow. It soon became the kitchen table in a one-bedroom apartment, where we ate our breakfast and planned our days. He to day care and I off to work was a grim reminder that all adventures are not necessarily of the pleasant kind. But I was young and had the wanderlust, so its effects didn't appear until years later.

Twenty-five years passed, and it stood in the corner of the basement of a high-priced colonial house, soon to be dug out again to hold all that was dear to me. I was alone this time, and it faced me, silent and empty, waiting for me to decide what was important and what was not.

I took it with me, but it was empty.

Its final destination was to the place where I am now, the final lap in a journey of a lifetime spent searching and wandering. Of course it was filled with what was true and good, mostly the memories of my children, adults now with suitcases of their own.

Which is what this column is really about.

They've all packed their suitcases in their own way and in their own time; it is the natural progression of things. But for the one whose journey had been interrupted, it was a tearful and joyous occasion to be packing at all.

My youngest daughter, Mary, left for New York City to finish college and to continue the final chapter of the story she has written, although only the beginning of her newest adventure.

"Come and see what I bought," she said to me, a sad smile on her face as I walked into her room for the last time. Her back to the window, she stepped aside to show me the item she had purchased to take her to her new life and forever severing her dependence on me.

A purple suitcase.

We looked at each other, eyes locked and the unspoken words hanging in the air like dew on the flowers. All the harsh words and the teenage fights melted away as the sun rose behind us, and we watched its ascension over the lake.

She was leaving for good this time and would not be coming back as the same person.

Her purple suitcase would be filled with her own memories, both the good and the bad, taking her where she needed to be.

It was empty. But I don't think it will stay that way for long.

SIT DOWN. YOU'RE
ROCKING THE BOAT

I was pregnant with my fourth child when we moved to Rochester, New York, in 1981.

Originally born in Brooklyn, raised on Long Island, I knew two things about Rochester. It was upstate near Canada, and it was cold, away from my family, my friends, and my job, away from the doctor who believed in drugs and not "natural childbirth," which I would soon experience here. Twice. I did not want to be here.

We were living here about a week when our only car, a mammoth 1976 Chrysler LeBaron, absolutely and without question died. The diagnosis was a new transmission, which cost $750. I was devastated. My husband could get to work on the bus; that was okay, but the car was my lifeline! How was I going to get to places, to Wegman's Supermarkets, to the bank?

Now, when I pray, I usually just talk out loud. If I am annoyed when I am praying, I am yelling out loud.

My family is used to this, but every now and then it would get a little embarrassing for them. Especially for my children when they were teenagers. If they had friends over and I was upstairs "praying" about something, they would say "Ah, Ma, we can *hear* you down here. He can still hear you if you whisper …" Or, "Are you talking to me or are you talking to God again?"

It was this wintry November morning in 1981 that I was praying to God for help in figuring out what to do next. Since it was Saturday, I should have been cleaning, but I was at such a loss. I was so angry.

"Okay, God," I started. "You brought me all the way up here to this frozen wasteland. You let me move away from all my family and my friends. You gave me all these kids, and now you are taking my car away from me? What am I supposed to do? Tell me what am I supposed to do."

Silence. Of course. I hadn't yet figured out that God works in his own time, not my time.

So I told my husband to watch the kids. I was going for a walk. Boy was I mad.

I walked and walked and finally found myself in front of a church. I went inside, not because I wanted to pray some more, but because I was cold.

The place was empty, and I sat up front near the altar. All of a sudden, this nun was sitting next to me. She could tell I was agitated, so she didn't say anything for a while. I guess she figured I was praying. Little did she know I was plotting my revenge because God had let me down for the last time.

Finally, she looked at me and said, "Can I help you, dear?" If looks could kill, I would have laid her out. "No, you can't help me, Sister. My car is trashed, I need $750 to fix it, and I don't have it. No, *you* can't help me. I'd really rather be left alone." And I dismissed her with a sniff and the flip of my hand that I am so good at doing.

She looked at me a minute, and then she said, "Wait right here."

Oh great, I thought. *Now I've done it. She's gone to get the priest.*

I was working my way out the rear of the church when she flagged me down, waving something in her hand. "Wait!" she yelled, as only a Sister of Mercy can scream. "Take this."

It was a check for $750! *Holy moley,* I thought, *She took money from the priest's desk! I better get out of here fast before he figures it out!*

So I ran down the street and into my house, where I showed my astounded husband the check that the crazy nun had given me. "We have to pay it back," I said, "but for now let's just get the car fixed."

So all winter long I scrimped and saved and put away as much money as I could so I would be able to pay that nutty nun back. Finally, as spring broke, I had met my goal.

I marched up to the rectory door and rang the doorbell. She answered, recognized me, and smiled. I looked at her, and with all my smugness, I announced, "Here I am, Sister, to repay you the money you gave me." I handed her the check and was ready to walk away, satisfied and proud that I had paid my "debt."

She held up the check, looked at it dramatically, and tore it in two, letting the pieces fall to the ground.

"I don't want the money back, Eileen," she said. Then she uttered the words that changed the course of my life. "Do good works."

She closed the door. I was standing there, stunned. Do good works? What the hell did that mean? I couldn't become a nun. I was married; I had kids for God's sake! What was she talking about?

I walked away in a daze.

It took a couple of years, but I eventually realized what she meant. I started to want to learn more about God. I became a Lector. I joined the choir. I became part of the Parish Council of my church. More and more each day, I learned about the goodness of God and his plan for me and how many times over I had been blessed.

As time went on, I realized that the nun wasn't crazy. She hadn't "stolen" the money from the priest's desk. Churches set up funds for people in need. I was in need more than she knew. She gave me a wonderful gift, worth more than $750 could ever cover. She gave me the gift of faith. She made me see that prayers are always answered, to be patient and to hold on tight when there is a storm. Because everything passes. You just have to hold on and believe.

Most importantly, she made me see that the world is bigger than me and my petty problems, the judgments I make of my fellow man, and the humanness of others. We're all here for a reason; we're all here to help each other. I pray for real now. Mostly they are prayers of thanksgiving and gratitude. But most of all, we are here to love. Each other and ourselves. And crazy nuns.

TO BE AND TO DO

The wind is roaring outside this morning as I sit by the window that looks out at the lake. Our lake; I can't help but think of it in any other way now.

The waves are pounding the shoreline as if it's the Pacific Ocean. I alternate between wonder and terror as I watch the white-caps appear and then get swallowed up as they break on the sand. Wondering at the immenseness of it all, I love the sound and wait for it each season. It lulls me to sleep on cold winter evenings when it's just me and the dogs at home. Oddly, the peace is mixed with terror if I think of how it could swallow me up if some freak of nature or God were to cause a tsunami. I close my eyes tight and concentrate on the dogs breathing in unison as they sleep, unaffected and secure. They are with Mommy, and it's all they care about at that moment.

My beloved's schedule and mine are different than when we first got together. I used to joke that I had to marry him in order to date him, for our work life consumed most of our daily life together. With my blessing, he finally retired to pursue his own dreams, and part of that dream involves travel.

The same has happened for me now, a year later. I "retired" from my job, which consumed much of my life, so much so I became very ill twice in the same winter season.

First with shingles (albeit a mild case, it was a nuisance just the same) and bronchitis, which blossomed into my first asthma attack. It was a serious wake-up call that I wasn't ready to heed.

I wrestled constantly with the notion of walking away from a terrific-paying job. It was realistic, but at what cost? I couldn't write at night; I was exhausted after putting in twelve-hour days, sometimes seven days a week. Church had become a distant memory, impossible to attend except for reading the Scripture together on Sunday mornings on weeks I didn't have to go in to the office. I rarely saw my kids or the grandchildren, and my friends were non-existent. It wasn't their fault—I simply didn't have the energy to even pick up the phone. Part of me felt very guilty, a feeling I was unable to shake or dismiss. I needed an answer and concentrated on finding the positive in what I had done.

This week I was offered a rare treat, to participate in a church service celebrating The World Day of Prayer. My attention was turned to the woman assigned to read aloud the passage of scripture from Luke 10:38–42. I realized as she read my heart should be at rest, and once again, I was where I was supposed to be, exactly where God had placed me.

My book sales are good, a fact I realize is part talent and mostly part luck, for I know that I write better every year than when I first began this journey of self-discovery and bleeding all over the page. I am finally purged and am ready to put to paper the real stories that live inside me and through me.

Newspaper work has been good to me as well, and picking up additional jobs affords me the freedom I crave and need to be creative. The best part is the recognition factor—someone recently asked for my autograph while we dined in a local restaurant; she had my book, and I was thrilled to do what she asked.

Signing her book with my smiling face on the back cover, I turned to my beloved and knew that God or karma or somebody was trying to tell me something.

As women, we are constantly reminded of our duality and that there are choices we can make. We can have it all but not all at the same time. I used to bemoan the fact that, although I was never sorry I had as many children as I did, I wished there was a way I could have pursued the dreams I had behind my eyes. I learned years later that it was not planned for me that way, and I can appreciate the successes more now that I am older. The story of Martha and Mary allows us to realize that we can be like, or indeed ought to be like, both of these women; we are to be and to do.

It's taken me my whole life to finally figure that out. I am so grateful I still have time to realize it. Let's make sure during this Easter season that we don't worry so much about the doing and just be. I have no idea where I will finally be laid to rest; it is my hope that it will be in the cemetery down the road. I can imagine us, my beloved and me, lying side-by-side as we watch the waves roll back and forth, the sounds lulling us eternally until we are ready to return for another adventure.

As Jesus and his disciples were on their way, he came to a village where a woman named Martha opened her home to him. She had a sister called Mary, who sat at the Lord's feet listening to what he said. But Martha was distracted by all the preparations that had to be made. She came to him and asked, "Lord, don't you care that my sister has left me to do the work by myself? Tell her to help me!"

"Martha, Martha," the Lord answered, "you are worried and upset about many things, but only one thing is needed. Mary has chosen what is better, and it will not be taken away from her."

Luke 10:38–41

THE HEART OF CHRISTMAS

Getting closer to the end of my life than nearer to the beginning, I am often beset with memories of days gone by, holidays and celebrations forefront in my mind. As it is the Christmas season, I am flooded with snippets of images, and my ears ring with old conversations.

Of course, I don't remember my first Christmas; in fact, there aren't many childhood occasions that spring forward to the space behind my eyes, beckoning to be called out and polished once again for the season.

But I do recall a Christmas where I was filled with envy and jealousy, a lethal combination in someone so short in experience and wisdom.

I had only received thirteen Christmas presents that year; I was insolent and spoiled enough to count them—how I must have hurt my parents to bemoan the fact there were *only* thirteen. I don't think I've ever given my children thirteen presents each for Christmas.

But there I was, crying and raging because I didn't get the doll I wanted—and my sister did. What an awful memory of Christmas to carry around with me, but I take it out year after year and remember how *not* to behave during the most high holiest of holy days.

My first Christmas as a working teenager was filled with pride and accomplishment. I had bought for my parents a decanter set, inlaid with gold and spun glass. A beautiful work of art to my uninformed eye, but to see it now I am amazed at how gaudy a creation it really was. Even thought they didn't drink wine, it sat on the dining room buffet, glaringly opulent in all its glory.

The first Christmas on my own was spent in a small apartment with a one-year-old baby, a son who was to learn quickly the value of love as opposed to monetary treasures—he truly was happy with a GI Joe and some small metal trucks. The first child always gets shorted somehow—it just seems to be the nature of life. But they are never shorted on love.

Children are the best part about Christmas, and I was blessed to have four and six at any given time, with friends and cousins also joining in the fray. It's part of the best memories of my life, and I wouldn't have done things differently if given the chance. Gifts were not as plentiful as in my childhood, but the time was taken to make sure it was what they wanted and what they could share. LEGO□ bricks and dollies, army men and Teenage Mutant Ninja Turtles, tea sets and jump ropes—the toys were intertwined and woven between them all, a way to connect and continue to grow as a family and as siblings.

My Christmas as a grandmother took on a whole new level of joy and depth of feeling. To see the creation that is part of you but not by you is amazing on so many levels.

But finally I come to this Christmas, when the emergence of new love and companionship was a gift to myself one Christmas morning several years ago.

The true meaning of the season is the gift we give to each other, the forgiveness toward a spoiled child who grew up to be a grateful woman—and the part of ourselves that is the most treasured.

Our hearts.

GOD'S FAVORITE SEASON

September.

Another new season is about to begin. Soon it will be time to put away that which is light and airy, to be replaced with the somewhat deeper hues of beiges, browns, and orange. Bright yellow makes way for softer mustard; voluminous red parts for calmer tawny greens and navy blues.

The colors of autumn. It is a time when the brilliance that lies within all of us is called forth. Bursting in the shower of hues we possess, the aromas and flavors like rainfall are as welcome as a comfy quilt on a cool fall evening.

The lake is translucent, the shimmering of diamonds on top the water. Rocks glisten in the path of the rays of the sun, calling us to listen one more time to the waves as they crash against the shore. As the tide goes out and in and out again, it reminds me that time does not stand still and does not wait for any being's command or plea to stop or slow its pace. The trees are bulging with fruit, begging to be harvested and relieved of the burden one more season. Time does not stop for heartbreak or disappointment, nor does it look the other way when one falls or is injured. Perhaps the balm to deal with such feelings is the changing of the seasons, for it reaffirms the continuity of life, the discipline of sameness, and the gift of renewal. Our lives are constantly changing, yet the undertow is constant.

September begins the new year for me, bringing back memories of the new school year, buying shiny new shoes and crisp white paper. January is more the halfway mark, as I look forward to the coming spring. Autumn has got to be God's favorite season. It reminds us that we are mortal, and our legacy is what we allow it to be. Give a long good-bye kiss to summer, and anxiously await her return next year.

GOD CAME TO TOWN

In a small town like this, in a church just like this one, a miraculous thing happened.

During the course of the praises and thanksgivings, between prayer concerns and discerning, a grandmother stood up and gave a couple a wonderful gift. Something they had been praying for the twenty years of their married life and for which they had accepted would be a joy they would never know.

They were childless and had no money to do as most others did. They could not afford to adopt and would not stoop to black market baby buying.

The old woman stood up among the congregation that sweltering summer day and asked a most poignant prayer. Her young granddaughter had given birth to a baby and was unable to care for it. They were not poor but not well off either.

"Does anyone want a child to love?" she asked as she stood tall after voicing her concerns.

"He's strong and he's healthy; he will be a fine young man one day."

The couple looked at each other and both stood up. No words were said.

None were needed.

Imagine going to church one day and coming home with a baby.

It happened.

In a small town like this, in a church just like this one, a miraculous thing indeed did happen.

God came to town and answered some prayers.

IT'S THAT TIME AGAIN

It is coming close to the end of yet another year, a time where I usually take stock of what I've done these past twelve months and what I might have done differently.

They say that hindsight is twenty-twenty, and that statement is truer now than ever before.

The older I get the more introspective I become but also more adept at letting go of what is not really important and holding tight to what is. I've written a lot about being a mother this year, and I'm not sure why. It's only a part of my life, a major part to be sure, but still, just a part of who I am.

Maybe it stems from watching my children enter the arena of adulthood and wanting to point out the pitfalls, the gullies they will step into if they are not careful. Although it is the flat plains of life I would like them to experience, it is just as important to experience the highs of the mountains and the loneliness of the deep caverns. Some of the goals I've set for myself have been met and surpassed while others sit waiting, like a lone apple on the top of the tree, waiting to be picked. It's been up there for quite some time and is no worse for wear in the waiting. Just like me. But I am realizing it is coming time to pick that last apple, to pluck from life all that is offered to me. I have done what I set out to do and await the challenge of what tomorrow may bring. I will face the future with my head held high, for I am proud of every step and misstep taken, for it defines who I am.

As I enter my fifty-fifth year, I will look upon it as a time of spiritual growth, awareness, and health expansion of a strong and sturdy body and soul. There are many good things in store for me and for all of us. I can't wait to see what tomorrow brings. How about you? You, dear reader, are part of who I am now, and what I am becoming. I enjoy meeting you, and nothing thrills me more to learn I've made you cry.

Old friends who have fallen away stay new with the memories of another time, and new ones emerge like poppies on the field, their aroma growing ever sweeter day by day.

May we always cherish the yesterdays, todays, and tomorrows before they are swept away like flowers in the wind.

HOLIDAY STORIES

A FAMILY LIVES HERE

One of my childhood fantasies was a recurring theme of holidays and decorating. When I was a grown-up, a mommy with babies and a house of my own, I would decorate with tablecloths and dishes appropriate for the season. Fancy silverware was used only at Thanksgiving, Christmas, and Easter, as was the same with all my little girlfriends who dreamt the same dreams of love, Prince Charming, and family.

The pièce de résistance would be two tall standing hutches, one of which was part of the dining room set and an unpainted but well-worn one in the kitchen.

It took close to thirty years to accumulate the Easter pastel napkins, the Halloween towels, the Thanksgiving tablecloth, and the Christmas lace, but I did. I was even able to enhance my collection to include red heart towels at Valentine's Day and green runners for St. Paddy's.

Part of the decorating process was to align the holiday dishes of the season on the kitchen hutch, complete with the appropriate tablecloths and other linens. I am amazed at how excited I still become when it is time to replace the dishes. If you ever want to buy me a present, get me a linen tablecloth and I am ecstatic.

My beloved is happy too because it's the only time I thoroughly clean the house. Vacuuming after three dogs is a daily occurrence, but this is different. It's like I get a fit of energy, a massive shock of activity that will not let me rest until the house is cleaned from top to bottom to showcase the newest holiday dishes. He bought me the hutches because he knew it made me happy, never realizing it was feeding an obsession.

After all the junk and knickknacks are dusted and washed clean, I stand back and admire my handiwork. I am done for the month, and it is time to move on to something else. I am reminded once again as it becomes more apparent year after year.

The simple things in life become the most precious, simply because they are.

But as long as I am able to reach the deep grooves in the hutch, there will be dishes there.

Sparkly clean and shiny, the display of old dishes proclaim, "A family lives here," just like my childhood fantasies.

I shall be content for the rest of my days.

THE GOOD FRIDAY BET

Every Easter season my children and I have this little ritual. It's called the Good Friday Bet, and it is simply this.

I bet them $10 that on every Good Friday, at 3:00 p.m., it will rain.

The first time I bet them, the youngest three were third, fourth, and fifth graders in Catholic school. It was something unique and different, a minor change in the routine, a new game to play. Their teachers got a kick out of it, and all eyes were on the sky when the time arrived.

Usually, I would lose.

I probably owe them about $10,000 each by now.

It was something they always forgot about until I would bring it up again, as soon as Lent started.

After a while they'd roll their eyes and say, "Okay, Mom, I'm in," knowing they never had to pay because the few times I did win, they offhandedly would remark, "I'll owe ya," as in the many times I "owed" them.

The entrance of high school brought a new dimension to the picture, for they were rebelling against more than just me and my beliefs. We didn't bet on Good Friday for several years.

Until one of my children went off to war.

"I thought of you and the Good Friday Bet," he wrote me shortly after that Easter. "I guess I owe you some money. Because it did rain here."

And that's what I wanted to impress on them all those years. All the times when I would grin and say, "Yup, you won again. I owe ya."

I'd hope that they would one day get it.

It always rains on Good Friday at 3:00 p.m. somewhere.

Just as every Easter Sunday he rose again.

Keep the money, son. I'll owe ya.

May you all have a happy and blessed Easter. Keep your eyes on the sky today. It's blue and clear, the promise of a wonderful day ahead.

Here.

THE EASTER TABLECLOTH

I have a faded pink and white tablecloth used only on Easter Sunday, and it has seen its share of meals over the years. I bought it new when I was a newlywed and thought to myself, *This should last a few years.* Ground-in Easter bread crumbs rolled in butter, tomato sauce, and red wine with dinner have graced it, as well as coffee rings and chocolate bunnies. It has survived food fights (not the good kind) and little fingers smashing hidden peas under plates. Yet it amazes me every time I take it from the linen closet; there are no telltale remnants of such stains, and even the largest of marks have faded away over time. There are few pieces of torn fabric only I can see, which would have no consequence to anyone else if they did notice it. It is the Easter tablecloth, and everything is right with the world. To my eyes, it is as clean as the cloth on the altar at church we attended those mornings when things were still black and white, priests were sinless, and there was no confusion about what was right and what was wrong. It was reborn every year.

We never seem to celebrate a holiday on its actual date in my family, and Easter this year was no different. The fact it came early made it especially tenuous for making travel plans, with snow still on the ground and icy windowpanes framing vibrant Easter flowers on the table. Easter in March is like eating ice cream in a blizzard; it just seems to blend in.

Our dinner was on Saturday this year, as traveling and work schedules made it so. We all met at my house on the lake—my children, their children, and me. Our thoughts were with my beloved, who was working out of town. He was missed.

A best friend of my sons also came out, always referred to as the fourth son, as well as someone new, a special friend of my daughter. They were driving up from Manhattan to "meet the mother"; it was a time of excitement and curiosity and catching up. Snuggling up with the grandkids and documenting the first new steps of the baby, it was a cozy if somewhat snug afternoon of cooking and drinking and laughing in the kitchen.

I've often wondered if they would ever really forgive me for divorcing their father, seemingly out of the blue to them but a necessity for my survival. It was a confusing time of anger, fear, and resentment, with acceptance only coming in short bursts of reality; this is how it is now and how it is going to be.

The next few years I tried to make the holidays as familiar as I could, with the same traditions and routines tying them to their old life while accommodating someone else who stood beside me. Things began to seem like they were in "the old days," but not quite.

It was time to gather in the big room, a room with different furniture and different seating arrangements than that of their childhood. The only thing familiar was the pink and white table-cloth on the dining room table.

"This is our Easter tablecloth," my daughter said to the one who makes her eyes shine and her smile as wide as her face will allow. "We've had it forever, and it still looks like new. It's as if it is reborn every year."

Yes, I thought to myself. *There are no telltale remnants of such stains, and even the largest of marks have faded away over time.*

Every Easter Sunday, we are forgiven; we are reborn.

It is the Easter tablecloth, and everything is right with the world.

Even on a Saturday in March.

ENTER THE PEACHES

There's nothing like a good bowl of peach cobbler.

When I first set out to make a pan of it, I realized how much I had missed eating it. For some reason I had fallen out of the habit of baking, and I suddenly remembered why. I'm not that good at it. No, the baking gene landed in the hands of my youngest daughter, who can whip up a carrot cake, a tiramisu, and a lemon chiffon pie without blinking an eye. Just typing those words makes me break out in a sweat, but it doesn't faze her in the least. I learned over the years, however, that I could impress dinner guests or hungry little mouths with a nice dish of hot apple, peach, or cherry cobbler. Mixing them together made me feel like a gourmet cook!

Adding ice cream atop the steaming crumbled mass of fruit and crunchy topping was an exercise in decadence.

"Wow, this is great! How did you learn to cook this good?" they'd ask, wanting to know the recipe for the exotic hot concoction. There are dozens of variations and different ways to serve it, but the ingredients were fairly simple: fruits, sugars, butter, flour, and love.

Pretty basic. I could handle that.

"It's a secret family recipe," I whispered and then pointed to my heart. Living in apple country these many years later has increased my affection for the cobbler. The seemingly unending supply of apples enabled me to bake to my heart's content. So many apples; it became so easy to make I became complacent, turning it into a routine dessert and not the special treat it once was. Enter the peaches. A peach cobbler was elegant and had a shorter season, marking the urgency of its arrival to the table. Its ingredients were the same, with love the final touch.

"Wow, this is great!" said my beloved as he spooned the sweet and sticky dessert into his mouth.

"Where'd you get this recipe?" I just smiled and tapped my heart again but also knew a lot more had gone into this recipe than in dishes past. Yes, there's nothing like a good bowl of peach cobbler, in all its delicious glory, and especially on cool autumn evenings such as these. I hope you enjoy eating it as half as much as I did making it. Sometimes the simplest recipes are the best.

APPLE CIDER MEMORIES

One of my favorite drinks is apple cider. You would think living in apple country would afford me the opportunity to drink it whenever my heart desires, but I don't. Apple juice can never be as extravagant as apple cider.

To my mind there's an unwritten rule we only drink it in the fall, at the beginning of harvest, draining our cups until the end of November. Ice cold with a molasses cookie on a brisk Saturday afternoon, or spicy hot as a mulled toddy on a cool autumn evening, my apple cider drink brings back memories of every color and stripe, thoughts of my youth, and the youth of my children.

When I was young, Halloween cookies frosted with orange icing and candy corn were the staples of my diet during that season, as was that of all my friends. There were no calories in those delectable treats that we worried over, no concerns as to sugar content and diabetic comas. I carried on the tradition with my children, who were only happy to oblige. While they were not indulged with sugary cereals or Kool-Aid, this was the season where concern over healthy eating went out the window. It is the stuff our memories are made of; between carving pumpkins and finding scary music to play, the sweet gobs of sucrose would stick with us like they stuck to our teeth, reminding us to stop only when it hurt to eat any more. Faces red with the cold on some Halloween evenings, we warmed ourselves with hot cider, a slice of orange, and a cinnamon stick. Trick-or-treat bags stuffed to the rim with candies and treats offered another chance of holding on to innocence and childhood.

Trick-or-treating was not only the signal of the end of the sugar highs but the turning of the page toward Thanksgiving. That holiday had treats all its own, with hot apple pies and mountains of vanilla ice cream or a giant block of cheddar cheese.

And a nice hot cup of apple cider. How very blessed we are to be part of the season of harvest and all that it brings us. May we never take it for granted or the farmers who share it with us.

LUMPS IN THE ROUX

With the approach of Thanksgiving, I am reminded of how things have changed.

When I was a young mother with babies and cats, the preparation for the holiday seemed to take days. Scouring the newspaper ads for the various sales at the competing supermarkets was a week-long event, culminating with the Sunday paper and its Pandora's box of colored flyers.

If I wasn't already confused by week's end, seeing the different prices for fresh cranberries and oranges, as well as bags of bread versus bagged, ready-made stuffing, I was close to the edge. Sweet potatoes or yams, mashed potatoes or baked, the choices were endless, daunting, but still a lot of fun. Canned cranberry sauce versus jellied? I could never decide, so I bought both. Corn, turnips, squash, I cooked it all, and there were enough leftovers to feed an army.

Of course the crowning glory was the turkey, with stuffing in it, around it, and behind it.

In my neighborhood, no self-respecting mother would serve a store-bought pie, but I always bought an apple pie to hide in the pantry, just in case my pumpkin pie was less than adequate. These were babies mind you, and if I smothered a "mistake" with whipped cream, no one was the wiser. But there were some people who kept score.

In fact, most imperfections could be hidden—dinner rolls whose bottoms were burnt could be cut off, creating "shorties." Mashed potatoes too lumpy? Add more butter. Better yet, one could drown the whole feast in gravy.

Gravy, too, could be bought in a can or ripped from a package. I came from a long line of gravy makers, and my mother made the best. She knew how to make it but didn't know how to teach me. Her heart laid more in matters of the arts, creative on canvas and clay but not in the kitchen.

My younger sister picked up cooking like a second language, and once she started talking, I was truly a foreigner.

So any time it came time to prepare a meal with gravy, my heart was heavy with the thought of messing it up once again. It was either too watery, too gooey, or too pasty. I tried and tried, but I just couldn't get it. It invariably turned out lumpy and uneven, a metaphor for the life I was living and trying not to notice.

Fast forward many years later, and although I had become more adept in the kitchen, gravies still intimidated me. As I entered a new stage in my life, that of a woman alone with no one to cook for or answer to, I began to experiment with recipes and theories, both *in* the kitchen and out.

I discovered the secret of the roux.

To seasoned chefs in the kitchen, this may come as quite a surprise that I had never learned the mastery of a skill so simple.

Roux: butter, flour, and pan drippings/juice from whatever you're cooking.

As I had with so many other areas of my life that year, I had to practice over and over and over again the roux, blending and stirring the three together until they are one. The roux has to become invisible, immersed into the gravy without taste and texture.

Because just as the roux is the foundation of any gravy, the substance you pour over your meal, so is the roux of life.

Love, tenderness, and kindness make the roux of a life one can be proud of and happy. They have to be blended to form the perfect base. There will be lumps if you don't have all three.

As with all the good things in my life, I have learned the secret of the roux. My foundation is now secure and the recipe is complete.

Everything else is gravy. Learn to make a perfect roux.

You'll never be sorry.

Happy Thanksgiving.

COOKIE EXCHANGE

As with most things in my life, it takes me a few tries to get it right.

Kids, jobs, marriages.

Cooking. Especially cooking.

So imagine my surprise when I was invited to a good old-fashioned Cookie Exchange.

"Come and bring four dozen of your own baked cookies," the invitation read.

Holding the green paper rimmed with gold, I read further.

"No store-bought allowed." I cringed.

Well, at least I can make a mean chocolate chip cookie, I thought smugly to myself. I continued.

"This is a Christmas Cookie Exchange, so no chocolate chip cookies either!"

Rats, I couldn't even bring my old standby.

Thank God for the Internet, Google, and the Food Network.

This was also going to be at a new friend's house, with an entirely new set of women whom I had never met or ever even talked to. I had heard her describe one or two, but for the most part, they were strangers to me and I to them.

"Here she is!" she said as I entered the room. My arms full with my plate of lopsided treasures, I was beckoned to add them to the already bulging table set with angels, bells, peffenuse, sugar cookies, and just about every other cookie you can imagine. They were beautiful.

I had made a rum-flavored orange lace cookie, a lemon sugar, a plain sugar, and fruit bundles, with homemade fruit stuff inside no less!

Needless to say, they were a hit, as no one would ever dare turn down a homemade cookie, no matter how chewy or doughy they may have turned out.

As I sat and looked at the beautiful display my new friend had set with all the varieties of cookies, I was once again reminded of how every day is a new day. A new chance to do something new or to do something you love all over again.

May your life always be filled with cookies. It is one of the reasons we are here.

No matter how lopsided or burnt, they tell the story of who you are.

Don't be afraid to whip up a new batch today.

CARDBOARD CHRISTMAS

Every year at this time I am reminded of the many blessings I have and the times where I thought I had none.

It was before the second husband, the onslaught of babies, and the beginning of a new awareness that my life was no longer my own.

I was the single mother of a three-year-old son and had moved to a new town. It was far away from where I was born and farther still from any family, friends, or outside influences.

I was twenty-three years old and mad at the world. God was a distant memory from junior high and certainly wasn't in my plans.

Having arrived with only our clothes and my young son's toys, I found a house close to work so that gas and parking wouldn't eat up what was left of already a meager salary. I had recently started a new job as a secretary in a small firm, qualifying for help with day care. Not welfare, but an adjustable rate charged against how much my salary totaled. It was enough to buy food and pay rent but not much else.

Time went by and we both made friends, although I didn't invite anyone over, since I had very little to entertain with. I didn't have a kitchen table, and the only bed was his; I slept on a mattress in the other bedroom. Our clothes were stacked neatly in cardboard boxes, our socks and underwear in plastic bins. My kitchen table was a purple suitcase. Christmas was coming, and I didn't have much in the way of funds, let alone a Christmas tree. I was invited to a cookie exchange, something even more foreign to me than learning to balance my checkbook. I respectfully declined.

My boss was a gruff old cuss, but as is usually with crusty types, he was a softie inside. He was a retired navy captain, and he would regale us with stories of his travels from all over the globe. He noticed a lot but never said much. Fridays were Bagel Day, a day when we would take turns bringing in bags of bagels and cream cheese for fellow workers to share, a time to stop and reacquaint ourselves and not just talk business. Whenever it came to be my turn, he would whisper to me, "I've got it this week." He noticed that I would always take an extra bagel and stuff it in my purse. He never drew attention to it except one time, to say conspiratorially, "For the boy?" and I would nod. "Yes. Thanks." It would be his treat after dinner, toasted and piled high with grape jelly.

Winter was in full blast in Pennsylvania, rumbling through the little town I had settled in like a locomotive on speed. Winters were damp and cold, and the wind chilled the bones so deep it is a memory that stays with me still. Snow was falling lightly the Christmas Eve of my memory, and I had wrapped the last of the three presents bought for my son with the money I had squirreled away. There was nothing else, no special dinner or plans for church. I was still mad at God for *putting* me in this mess.

Putting my young one to bed, we talked excitedly about Santa and his expected arrival, for I didn't want to dampen his mood or lessen his childhood joy of the season. I had cut a small tree down from the neighboring park, and it sat in the corner of the living room, minus lights or Christmas balls, just some silver tinsel I had gotten for ten cents a package. Stuffed in a cardboard box to hold it up, it stood there looking as forlorn as I had felt.

I sat on the deep sill of the kitchen window, watching the flakes fall against the backdrop of the streetlights. It was early evening and the TV was silent, a small black and white portable that also sat on a cardboard box. It was quiet and snow muffled any sound, except for the crunch of tires on the street below.

I thought about the choices I had made that had put me in this position. Although I was tired, I was calm because I knew that I had done the best I could for my child, and that was what was really important to me. I knew that my time would come, but it would be a long time coming. It was then that I started to think about God again and what I needed to do to make things right with him, to raise my son with morals and stability.

Eventually I became lost in my thoughts and feeling sorry for myself. My eyes didn't immediately focus on the truck that had stopped in front of my house. It wasn't until I noticed the figure below waving its arms excitedly that I realized I was looking at the face of my boss and some coworkers. The crusty old man was beaming from ear to ear, and the doorbell rang loudly. My son ran from the bedroom asking, "Is Santa here?"

Running to the front and pulling the door open, I saw them standing there, holding chairs and end tables, a stainless steel kitchenette set, and a mattress with a headboard and frame. They smiled silently as they walked past me and laid them down in the appropriate rooms.

One by one, they quietly placed them down, looking around the sparse rooms that were clean but empty. Box upon box of dishes, silverware, and linens piled up in corners of the kitchen, until finally they were finished. They had cleaned out their attics, their cupboards, and their wallets, also surprising me with a cooked turkey with all the trimmings.

They stood in my little living room, eleven in all. Coworkers with spouses, they stood waiting, never uttering a sound.

The crusty old man gave the cue, and they began to sing.

"We wish you a Merry Christmas, we wish you a Merry Christmas, we wish you a Merry Christmas, and a Happy New Year. Merry Christmas!" they shouted, and only then did I let the tears flow. Full of gratitude and love for my fellow workers, I never forgot the feeling they gave me. I relive it every year at this time, and I give freely to others. I don't think they knew the depth of their kindness and how much it touched me.

Two years after that, I remarried and spent a lot of years raising a family. I have been rich and I have been poor, but I have never forgotten the joy that comes with giving as well as receiving. I have thanked God for being and experiencing both.

Thank you to all of you, wherever you are now. Your gift was much more than you'll ever know.

Merry Christmas to those who have and those who have not.

No matter what you have, share it with others.

THE BROWN BLANKET COAT

Originating from Long Island, a stone's throw away from New York City, I consider myself to be a woman of keen fashion sense, flair, and style. I will openly admit I am very much a snob when it comes to the clothes I will wear. Garments hawking Donna Karen, Bill Blass, Anne Klein, and Ralph Lauren were what I most preferred. I entered young adulthood nourished by a steady diet of the most expensive designer labels and products. I only bought the best, and if I didn't have the money, I would save my pennies until I did. Classic designs and lines (with matching shoes and handbags) were the mantra of my day.

As a result, I have been rewarded with a wardrobe that has withstood the test of time and has lasted through many dry cleanings and raising many children. Classics never go out of style, and good fabric is indestructible. Which is why I surprise everyone every late fall, when the chill winds turns to winter snow, and I look in my closet for my winter coats.

There is it again. The ugliest coat I have ever seen.

It's a brown, houndstooth pattern, double-breasted, mid-length wool coat. It cost $75 in 1987. Every winter since then I look at this monstrosity hanging in my closet, haul it out, and make myself wear it for several days as the chastisement from my daughters and friends begins. It's become a tradition, and they think it's all a big joke. If they only knew.

"What were you thinking?" I hear over and over. "Oh, not *that* coat again! It's so eighties! It has no lines, no pleats. It has no collar and no fur. No cuffs, no silk lining, and no gold buttons. It's a plain, black buttoned, rayon-lined blanket!" I smile. Fashion diva that I am, I still will not allow myself to part with this coat.

For they don't know the story.

Many years ago, Sunday mornings were spent going to church together as a family. There we would be, the seven of us, going down the aisle to our seats, taking up a full pew. I would be so proud of my little ones, all dressed in matching jackets or identical sweaters, baby girl in a little fake fur hat muffler. Praying was secondary; I was all about "showing off" my brood.

Their father and I would be dressed in our Sunday best. Because of our large family, finances were tight and our best didn't always look that great. Our coats were never dirty or torn but would look old and worn, having seen better days. His looked worse than mine. Of course his things always looked worse than mine. He never bought himself anything and wouldn't accept a gift from me. That's the kind of man he was.

An older woman used to sit alone in the pew behind us. She would always give us a big hug and kiss at the beginning of worship. She usually had a sucker or piece of chocolate that she would sneak to the kids for "after church." When it came time to give me a hug, Dorothy would inevitably first look at my coat, then sigh, and then look at my husband with a look to say, "Can't you get her something decent?"

I know it always made him feel funny, but we never discussed it.

One Sunday in October, when the leaves were just about off the trees, Dorothy surprised me with a gift out in the church parking lot. It was a mink coat, a *real* mink coat, one that had obviously been of excellent quality to have lasted so long. The buttons were worn, some of the clasps were torn off, and there was a tear at one of the seams. It had been her coat when she was younger.

"I know it needs a little tailoring," she said, pulling me closer so no one else could hear, "but it's better than what you have now. Get it fixed. No one needs to know I gave it to you." She headed toward the church entrance to sit back in her seat and began saying her rosary, smiling, content she had done the "right thing."

"Ahh … thanks," I stammered, not really knowing what to say. I had never had a fur coat. We couldn't afford one, and it would be some time before he would be able to even think of getting me one. My grandmother had a black mink that my mother borrowed now and then. I remember rubbing my hands on it the one or two times a year she would wear it. I had the same feeling now as when I felt grandmother's coat. Envy. After Mass and getting in the car, I couldn't look at my husband. Neither could he look at me.

Several days went by as I struggled with my conscience.

I wanted to run out to a furrier and get those latches secured.

I wanted to get it steam-cleaned and have the torn lining sewn back in.

I wanted to wear that coat.

But I knew that if I traded it in for money, I could get $300 for it. Three hundred dollars could buy groceries for a month. Toys for Christmas. A coat for my husband.

Or I could get a new coat for myself.

When I left the furrier with the money in my hand, I was torn as to what my next step should be. As I turned the corner, I tried to convince myself that I was the one who the coat money should be spent on, not the kids, not the family.

Dorothy gave that coat to me, I reasoned. *I deserve a new coat! I work so hard, have all this responsibility, and I haven't bought myself something nice in years. Why shouldn't I take this money and get myself an expensive leather jacket?*

My question was answered when I turned the next corner.

God doesn't waste any time; another one of those defining moments.

It was a beautiful winter afternoon, and people were walking up and down the street, enjoying the day and chattering in their own little worlds. As I got to the end of the corner and was about the cross the street, the light turned red. I had to wait. I looked over to my left and saw a parked car.

A 1979 Rambler. Brown. It was full of papers and clothes and books. In it was a woman close to my age and what looked to be two young girls, around seven and eight years old. Several coloring books were stacked on the dashboard.

What a mess, I thought.

Until I looked again.

The kids were sleeping close together in the backseat, dirty blankets pulled up to their chins. The woman had her head on the steering wheel, softly crying. The mess that surrounded them was every possession they had in the world.

They were living in that car.

In the midst of all the activity of this beautiful day was a family living in a car.

How many times had I passed them and didn't notice?

All I knew was I didn't have a nice coat.

Before I could change my mind, I knocked on her side of the car. Barely allowing the window to be rolled halfway down, I threw the $300 through the small slit and choked out, "Merry Christmas."

I turned and walked away quickly, ashamed. What had I become?

Several days later, I bought the brown, black-buttoned, houndstooth-patterned, blanket coat on sale for $25, marked drown from $75.

It is the ugliest coat I've ever seen, but I wear it at least for a week during the winter.

Not to remind myself that I did a "good deed" and gave the woman some money. God knows she needed more than the $300. Not as a clarifier that I was an unselfish person and thought of someone else.

I keep it to remind myself that I had felt the other way.

Greedy, entitled, and selfish—I never wanted to feel that way again.

Now, I am not going to pretend I am a martyr and wear nothing else but that coat. I'm not saying I won't try to find the next "gottahave" dress or forgo the whole shopping experience of scooping out the perfect shoes.

But I will keep the brown blanket coat forever. I will never get rid of it. There but for the grace of God, go I.

Life can change in a moment. I don't know what the circumstances were to force the woman and her kids to live in their car. I didn't want to know.

But I keep the brown blanket coat as a warm reminder.

When I start getting cocky, I remember the coat. I still want nice things, but I will never get rid of that coat, and I will never put things before my family.

There but for the grace of God.

WAITING BY THE WINDOW—A
CHRISTMAS STORY FROM THE LAKE

The two brothers sat side by side, watching the snowflakes as they fell in big clumps, piling up right in front of them. The big bay window seemed like a widescreen TV, and they loved to watch the cars go by every morning as Mommy and Daddy went about their day.

But today was Saturday, and everyone was home, scurrying every which way to get things done. It was Christmas Eve, and the boys knew that soon the good smells would be filling the kitchen of the little house they lived in.

Daddy had lugged the tree up from the basement. It stood upright in the same corner as it always did. The brothers loved to watch the twinkling lights and the shiny ornaments as they sparkled during the evening hours. They would lie on their backs on either end of the comfy couch, silent and content as Mommy hung the last of the candy canes, listening to the Christmas music playing softly on the radio.

Do you think we can sneak one? The older brother winked to the younger.

Do we dare? the young one whispered excitedly, and they brushed against the tree gently to make one of them fall silently to the ground. Munching it quickly, they shared the sweet, even though they knew it would never be missed, as there were many, many more throughout the tree.

Coming up from the basement with the last of the boxes in his hand, their father smiled to himself as he watched them lick their lips to get the last of the peppermint chips.

His face fell slightly as he spied the little box within a box, hidden unknowingly so as not to remind them. The box that had once held an ornament he and his wife had purchased together, one of the few gifts they had gotten for each other for their first Christmas together. It was plain, a sparkly snowman that had hung from their tree for many years.

Suddenly it was gone, and they never knew what had happened to it. They surmised it must have fallen from the Christmas tree during the hustle and bustle of opening presents, mistakenly thrown out among the wrapping paper. It was a sad reminder that sometimes bad things just happen.

"Better not let your mother see you do that," he said conspiratorially, and they nodded in agreement. Besides, it was time to get back to the window. They had an important job to do and didn't want to mess it up.

I wonder what he'll bring us, the younger one said to the older.

Who? he answered with mock innocence, knowing full well who his brother was talking about. He loved to tease him because it was so easy.

Who? his brother screamed and then calmed himself. He didn't want Mommy to know they were getting excited. They didn't want to have to leave the window and not witness his arrival.

Who? he whispered now, almost to himself. *You know who!*

Yes, I know, I know! the older brother answered, the enthusiasm of the younger contagious.

I can't wait for Mommy and Daddy to see what we got them! he said suddenly, and his brother nodded excitedly in agreement.

They sat there all day, in front of the big bay window, and watched with hearts pounding, their eyes darting from corner to corner as the snow continued to come down, coating the cars and the tops of hats worn by those who passed by.

They were becoming sleepy, the dim of the afternoon becoming night, the lights of the tree shining brighter and brighter. Their eyelids were getting heavy, and long, dry yawns began to escape from their mouths. Try as they might, they were no longer able to keep their heads up, and they lay on the carpeted floor in front of the window.

It will be okay, the older said to the younger as they snuggled up together, the warmth of each other's bodies calming their quickly beating hearts.

Let's just stay here until we hear him … the younger said as he drifted off to sleep.

Yeah, until we hear him … And soon they both were snoring lightly, a slow and rhythmic breathing that comes from the sleep of knowing you are loved.

Mommy and Daddy stood together, their arms wrapped around each other, smiling at the two brothers who lay contently on the floor.

"I wonder what dogs dream of," Mommy said sweetly, kissing the side of Daddy's cheek.

"I hope they dream of Santa Claus, just like everyone else," he said simply and kissed her back.

"Merry Christmas, boys," they whispered and walked toward the staircase and upstairs to their bed.

They left the two sleeping dogs in front of the big bay window, who dreamt the dream of children, of wrapping paper, presents, and St. Nicholas.

The slept close together, both of their furry paws protecting their gift for Mommy and Daddy, a gift of love and adoration for those they cherished.

A white snowman ornament they had found in the dirt, just the day before.

Merry Christmas!

THE BEST IS YET TO COME

It is New Year's Eve, and I am listening for the phone with one ear while I make the bed and start the laundry. Not to see if I have a date or not—that's a given now, although my date of the evening is down for the count with a sinus infection. One of my favorite parts of telling the story of how we got together is that "I had to marry him to be able to date him," since our work schedules were so chaotic back then.

We had planned to go to dinner down the road to celebrate with the rest of the grateful, but it looks like that might be on the back burner. Instead, I'll most likely be watching the remnants of my youth on the TV as I once again view an aging Dick Clark. America's youngest teenager is looking a little rough around the edges the last few years, but he still feels it's his responsibility to count down the old and bring in the new. My beloved will snore beside me, sleeping the dreams of drug-induced slumber while the germs beat a hasty retreat, dissipating into the fog of the vaporizer laced with Vick's vapor rub.

It's nice to feel needed, which I think is what drives the teenager as well.

I'm waiting for the phone to ring, telling me if I have to come into work. If it doesn't ring for today it most likely will be for tomorrow—and that's okay. It's the unknown that's a little disconcerting. But for the most part, I am happy to be home, writing some thank-you notes, organizing my office for the new year, and tending to my sweet, ailing hubby.

There is no longer the daily list of check-ins to see where my children might be. I already know. They are where they are supposed to be.

No more are the calls to find out who is sleeping over at whomever's house, or who the designated driver is, or who is buying the beer. It's no longer any of my business, although they have all connected in one way or the other to wish us a Happy New Year. Time has passed to allow such mundane checklists to float away like the vaporizer mist in my bedroom.

The phone hangs on the wall in the kitchen, and I once again spy the most beautiful apron in the world. Given to me by my son and his beloved, it is truly a gift made from the heart. I received it on our Saturday Christmas and immediately tied it around my waist, christening it with tomato sauce and ham juice. It will pain me to have to wash it, to remove the newness of it. For now, it will hang on the doorjamb of my kitchen, a constant reminder of their appreciation of becoming a family. I would frame it if I could.

All of them worked on it, my oldest grandson and even the baby christening it with their perspiration, late-night fatigue, and love. All of them ailing with the bug now visiting my beloved, they worked until their eyes were heavy with sleep and fevers too high to ignore.

From the tiniest sewing of gingerbread men appliqués on the front to mending the raw edges of the tiebacks, it is probably one of the most touching gifts I have ever received. It will become the touchstone to my performance as a mother-in-law, a reminder to bite my tongue when I don't agree with something or to praise when I am happy.

The sun is falling behind the clouds as it will soon begin to snow again, something the weathermen had forecasted and is not a surprise. It is December 31, and I am once again reminded of how blessed I have been and how much I am looking forward to the new year.

I look forward to another year of writing about this community and to share with the readers who frequent my columns my thoughts of the day or share a story or two. It is what I was always meant to do, and becoming a writer is one of my proudest accomplishments. There are several books being released this coming year.

So I will continue to look forward and not back. I won't wallow in self-pity or remorse. Most of all, I will remember the message from my dad, the off-the-cuff remark left on a recorded message of good-bye to my mother and my siblings and most pointedly to me. He must have recorded it on one of his good days and hid it so as not to be found until many years later.

Ephesians 4:31–32, "Get rid of all bitterness, rage and anger, brawling and slander, along with every form of malice. Be kind and compassionate to one another, forgiving each other, just as in Christ God forgave you."

Happy New Year!

BAND OF BABIES

When my kids were little, there wasn't a lot of money for things other than necessities. Every now and then there would be a dollar or two left over that I could use to buy something really cheap, like a jump rope or jacks with a small rubber ball.

We were broke but happy. They never knew anything was different.

After the first baby, they seemed to come in succession, one being born right after the other. It seems as if I had just laid one down on the floor to roll around with the others when another one took its place in my arms.

Being born so close together gave them camaraderie still evident today. They have so many memories of their childhood, as do I, and holiday times are a special time to rejoice and remember when things were different and sometimes simpler.

I spent most of my time in the kitchen, whether it was doing dishes (no dishwasher), doing laundry (no dryer), or tending to little ones. Since there were more babies than I had arms, they inevitably ended up on the floor.

One of their favorite toys to play with was the pots and pans under the sink. A long wooden spoon and a few plastic measuring cups created a symphony that only a mother could love or appreciate. Misshapen and mismatched pot covers and plastic Tupperware strewn all over the kitchen floor; how I wish I had taken a picture. My memory will have to do.

I can still see them in my mind's eye, toothless grins and open mouthed like little birdies waiting for dinner. The delight when they all ended up playing in rhythm, a brigade band of babies marching nowhere, their joy utterly palpable.

Although I still have the set of pots and pans, at this point in my life I am able to afford pretty much whatever I want. I am looking forward to purchasing a new set of pots, complete with matching utensils and lids.

But I am thinking of laying them all out on the floor, just one more time.

The grandkids are coming over, and I need to hear some music.

EPILOGUE

There are still many more columns to read, for I will continue to write them as long as I am able.

If you'd like to read more online, my Web site is: www.eileen-loveman.blogspot.com

I hope that I have touched you in some small way with my musings and caused you to look at things in a new way or to remember feelings long past.

And if I made you cry, I did my job.